TRADE UNIONISM

TRADE UNIONISM

Three main aspects of trade unionism are examined in this book —collective bargaining, pressure group politics to achieve social change, and democratic participation in the government of trade unions. Each of these aspects is studied in Great Britain and, comparatively, by reference to a critical case in another society. Thus British collective bargaining is compared with the system in Russia and Jugoslavia, British welfare unionist politics with business unionism in America, British trade union democracy with rank-and-file union participation in ex-colonial Africa. In this way the author demonstrates the essential features of the British system and is able to draw some general conclusions about possible trade union developments in the future. Throughout, the approach is sociological and the book is designed to show how a comparative analysis illuminates features of the trade union movement which could otherwise be obscured by the volume of detail accrued by each given case.

THE AUTHOR

J. A. Banks studied sociology at the London School of Economics from 1947 to 1952; his M.A. thesis, based on a research project was later published as *Prosperity and Parenthood* (Routledge and Kegan Paul, 1954). He lectured in sociology at Leicester until 1954 when he left to join the industrial sociology research team, led by W. H. Scott, at the University of Liverpool. As research lecturer and senior research lecturer he was engaged in a wide range of industrial and other research, publishing (with Scott, Halsey and Lupton) *Technical Change and Industrial Relations* (Liverpool University Press, 1956) and *Industrial Participation* (Liverpool University Press, 1963), as well as numerous other books and articles. He is now professor of sociology at the University of Leicester.

THEMES AND ISSUES IN MODERN
SOCIOLOGY

Trade Unionism

J. A. BANKS

COLLIER-MACMILLAN PUBLISHERS
LONDON

Collier-Macmillan Publishers
Cassell & Collier Macmillan Publishers Limited, London
35 Red Lion Square, London WC1R 4SG
Sydney, Auckland, Toronto, Johannesburg

The Macmillan Publishing Co. Inc.
New York

Library of Congress Catalogue Card Number: 73-17755

First printing 1974

ISBN 0 02 972170 9 (cased)
     0 02 972180 6 (paperback)

Printed in Great Britain by
Northumberland Press Limited, Gateshead

CONTENTS

CONCLUSION

CHAPTER I

The Sociology of Trade Unionism

Trade unions and trade unionists face a crisis in their affairs at the present time. More successful than they have ever been before in their relations with employers, they confront an ambivalence on the part of their countrymen which is difficult to live with and apparently even more difficult to dispel. On the one hand, they are recognized, and even reluctantly admired, for being a power in the state, capable of protecting themselves from the caprice of impersonal market forces and setting an example to others not so well organized and co-ordinated as they. On the other hand, they are feared as a threat, because they are felt to exacerbate chronic inflation and weaken the economy through the ease with which they drive home wage demands on unwilling but relatively quiescent businessmen and administrators. Traditional economic and political modes of analysis seem to provide no satisfactory account of their nature and circumstances, save in the sense of hastily erected explanations for each new event as it occurs. Nostrums abound, of course, for putting the trade union house, and the economy generally, into good working order; but the significance of events, especially in the context of long term developments, eludes comprehension, so that each fresh 'remedy' rapidly follows its predecessors into oblivion.

Where others so regularly fail, the sociologist may perhaps be forgiven for not attempting the apparently impossible; but the twentieth century is the century of sociology, and advocates of the discipline would be shirking their responsibilities were they not to meet the challenge of the times in their own terms. The argument of this book, therefore, is primarily that the sociological framework of analysis enables people to see any social phenomenon in its context, and hence provides them with the basis of assessment for action. Trade unionism will accordingly be examined here by reference to those types of sociological enquiry which seem relevant to the matter in hand, and the various facets of the organized behaviour of groups of employees will be considered in much the same manner as that which sociologists employ when they study what are apparently very different phenomena.

Historically speaking, there have been two contrasting ways in which trade unions have been located in society by those who have studied them. The first, associated with the names of Lujo Brentano (1870) and George Howell (1878) in the nineteenth century and Frank Tannenbaum (1952) in the twentieth, has concentrated on the features which trade unions share with the craft guilds of the Middle Ages. The nature of the division of labour which separates carpenter from weaver, fisherman from farmer, is what is seen as significant from this point of view. The Trade Union, like the Guild, is regarded as an association, reflecting the similarity of outlook and sense of community of all who follow the same trade or occupation, and the expectation of students of this persuasion is that wherever technical or other developments bring about a re-organization of work, new associations will appear to foster the spirit of solidarity amongst workers which has been temporarily destroyed. It is 'an historical law' claimed Howell (1891) that wherever men suffer from the break-up of an old order they seek to maintain their independence by creating a new one. Thus, the trade unions were a product of the industrial revolution in very much the same sense as the craft guilds were a product of the struggle of the artisan to free himself from control by the medieval town lord. Both craftsmanship and industrial employment are of such a nature that men, labouring at a common task, inevitably develop a sense of identity which marks them off from others, labouring at different tasks.

The alternative view, best exemplified in the work of Sidney and Beatrice Webb (1894), although also shared by many other scholars, emphasizes that trade unions are historically specific, a product of the economic and social conditions of no more than a particular phase of human civilization. The Webbs, especially, believed the contrast between their own and the former point of view to be so crucial that they began their history of trade unionism with a discussion of the *differences* between the trade unions and guilds, laying distinctive emphasis on the lack of historical continuity in the organization of workers in the same calling from medieval to modern times. 'We assert, indeed, with some confidence,' they wrote, 'that in no case did any Trade Union in the United Kingdom arise, either directly or indirectly from a Craft Guild.' Some possibility remained, they thought, that organizations of journeymen could have provided the basis for subsequent trade unionism in their occupations, but direct link with the guilds could not be traced. There was in the Webbs' minds a very sound reason for this, namely the *structural* difference between guild and trade union. The 'central figure' in the former, 'in all instances, and all periods of its development' was the master craftsman who owned the instruments of production and sold the product. Thus, 'the typical guild member was not wholly, or even chiefly, a manual worker. From the first he supplied not only whatever capital was needed in his industry, but also that knowledge of the markets for both raw material and product which is the special function of the *entrepreneur*. The economic functions and political authority of the guild rested, not upon its assured inclusion of practically the whole body of manual works, but upon the presence within it of the real directors of industry of the time.' By contrast, the central figure in the trade union movement is the employee, typically a manual worker, owning neither the raw materials, nor the means of manufacture, nor the final commodity he produces. Employers, who do in fact own the instruments of production and the product of their employees' labour, are outside the trade unions altogether, and, where they have organizations of their own, they expect them to protect their interests in direct conflict with those of the men they employ.

Indeed, for the Webbs, the possibility of historical continuity from associations of journeymen to the modern trade union arose from the very contrast between their situation as *permanent* employees and that of the apprentice who was usually the son of a master craftsman himself and, if not always certain to marry his master's daughter, might reasonably hope to become a master himself one day. As soon as there appeared on the historical scene a *lifelong* class of wage servants who, within a few years of ceasing to be an apprentice, were unable to accumulate sufficient capital to set themselves up in business in their own right, the basis was laid for trade union action, as opposed to guild organization. The society in which trade unions flourish may thus be said to be divided horizontally. Employees in different industries have interests in common to protect against their employers, who direct the processes of production in their own interests. By contrast, medieval industry was divided vertically in that all who pursued a craft had a common interest, whether as master, journeyman or apprentice, to prevent outsiders from encroaching upon their practices.

The difference between the historically specific and the historically general conceptions of trade unionism must, however, not be regarded as a simple matter of truth versus error. Rather is it a consequence of contrasting emphases on the dissimilar as opposed to the similar ways in which men have gone about the business of working together to produce things. Trade unions *are* like guilds to the extent that they protect the economic interests of their members against those who are seen to threaten them. Irrespective of the particular historical form, that is to say, the division of labour in any epoch carries with it the implication of a division of economic interest, and therefore of conflict between interest groups. Wherever master craftsmanship dominated, such a conflict of interests manifested itself in craft guilds, linked together with other bodies, such as merchant guilds, to form an urban complex, the so-called 'plebeian' city (Weber, 1958) marked by exclusiveness from the world outside and by internal, political struggles. The relations between the separate craft guilds in a town community were often far from harmonious, especially over the question of 'the demarcation of their industrial spheres. It was a difficult task to draw a sharp line between allied occupations, and the craft guilds jealously resented any attempts at what they regarded as a usurpation' (Lipson, 1947).

Where capitalism prevails, such demarcation disputes also arise between trade unions, but they are overshadowed by the wider pervading conflict of interests between trade unions and employers or employers' associations. Sociologists emphasize that such conflicts of interest do not, however, necessarily result in the destruction of the parties, no more than the earlier conflicts led to the destruction of the guilds. Both sides in a conflict continue to exist for a long time and will continue to do so, so long as there is some advantage to them both in the persistence of the relationship. Thus, under capitalism, trade unions and employers' associations are linked to form what is usually referred to as an industrial relations *system*, the characteristic feature of which is *collective* bargaining between the buyers and sellers of labour power within a labour market. Clearly, an essential feature of the sociological analysis of trade unionism is the sociology of such industrial relations systems, and the first part of this book is, accordingly, devoted to this subject.

At the same time, the emphasis on the historically specific argument that collective bargaining under capitalism is a very different kind of activity from the essentially political nature of guild conflict, which was contained by the power of the municipal authorities, should not be interpreted cursorily to mean that within a given, historical period an industrial relations system experiences no history of its own. When trade unions are first formed they can depend upon the loyalty of a small fraction only of all the people whose occupations they have been set up to protect. If, and as, they establish themselves as effective bargaining bodies, the proportion of potential members who become actual members increases. In sociological terms they become more *complete*. Over a period of time, too, their activities broaden in scope and deepen in intensity. Trade unions may thus become, in Blackburn's terminology, more *unionate*; that is, more committed to what have come to be regarded as the general principles and ideology of trade unionism. In the British context at the present time, for example, such unionateness on the part of the trade union entails:

(1) regarding collective bargaining and the protection of the interests of union members against employers as its *main* function.
(2) remaining *independent* of employers for purposes of negotiation.
(3) being prepared to use *all* forms of industrial action, including strikes, to achieve its aims.
(4) declaring itself to be a trade union.
(5) registering itself as a trade union.

(6) affiliating itself to the Trades Union Congress.
(7) affiliating itself to the Labour Party (Blackburn, 1967).

Sociologists may, of course, follow Blackburn in using completeness and unionateness as separate indices of unionization, and the more general concept as the measure of the social significance of an individual trade union at any moment of time. The notion of unionization is obviously capable of extension to the even more general idea of the character of trade unionism as a social movement, indicating what such a movement is ideologically committed to achieve and what it has so far succeeded in achieving. The emphasis of trade unionism as a social *movement*, that is to say, draws attention to the collective endeavour on the part of trade unionists, within their separate unions and in co-operation between unions, to bring about some significant *change* in their situation, and even more broadly, so to alter the economic and social systems in which they find themselves that they take another form, regarded as more desirable. Blackburn's seven characteristics of unionateness are the dimensions of their operations to this end in the British context up to the present time. Thus, trade unionism cannot be understood merely in terms of trade union participation in an industrial relations system, because the nature of that system itself experiences modification to the degree that trade unions are successful in their efforts to modify it. Of course, there are other reasons why industrial relations systems change —and the student of these systems ignores them at his peril— but insofar as this book is concerned with trade unionism as such, and therefore with the trade union side of the collective bargaining process rather than with the employers' side, the focus of attention is necessarily directed towards the mobilization of trade unionists over a period of time to realize a more comprehensive series of goals than is implied by the concept of economic interests. From the sociological analysis of the industrial relations system, therefore, the second part of this book turns to consider the nature of the trade union movement.

Social movements, however, are usually thought of by sociologists as comprising two broad classes of persons, (a) *members* of organized bodies with fairly specific aims and purposes to which these members subscribe, and (b) *adherents* to such ideas, whether they are expressed by the members of such organizations, where they exist, or find currency in a society more diffusely, where they do not. In antiquity and in the Middle Ages there is evidence of unrest and protest by slaves and other workers (Beer, 1957); and it is even possible that there were embryonic labour movements in the sense that craftsmen and others adhered to certain views of the system of production of their time and had dreams about a different kind of social order, more consonant with their beliefs about the dignity of labour and the destiny of mankind. But it was not until the journeymen began to organize their exclusive 'Companies' and, more particularly, not until the trade union movement appeared, that *membership* became the overwhelmingly significant feature of this aspect of industrial life rather than *adherence*. The distinction is between an organized labour movement, possibly with penumbra of outside supporters, and one which merely mobilizes adherents spasmodically and never achieves the kind of long-term incorporation which the modern concept of organization implies. Notwithstanding the regular loss of old members and gain of new ones, a trade union persists in maintaining a corporate entity marked by distinctive aims and objects and by a characteristic mode of consolidating its membership. What the Webbs called 'a continuous association of wage-earners' (1894)—a conception which today we may expand to include also salary-earners—admits to membership only people who it may legitimately regard as equals, by virtue of their employment in a particular 'trade', however loosely this is defined. Such an association is self-designated as a union of equals, democratically organized; and it is of some sociological significance to examine the extent to which trade unions are able to maintain such a democratic ideology in practice, when they participate in an industrial relations system with employers who do not necessarily subscribe to such values. The third part of this book examines this question in the broader context of the sociology of democratic organization.

Of course, the distinction between the historically general and the historically specific approaches to the study of trade unionism is one example merely of the wider methodological issue of where a student is to draw the line when he is analysing social phenomena. Not everything can be studied at once, if ever, and some aspects of the phenomena in question must be disregarded, in order that others, deemed more central, may be given their due attention. Selection between possibilities is therefore inevitable, although a major source of misunderstanding may be avoided by making the motif underlying the selection quite clear. In the present instance the three parts which follow illustrate how a sociologist uses sociological concepts and theory to illuminate a problem area. The first chapter in each part takes up, in order, the three aspects of trade unionism outlined above, industrial relations systems, trade union movements, democratic organizations, considered generally. The next step in every case is to apply this general analysis to the specific conditions of collective bargaining, the trade union movement, and trade union democracy in Britain. The third chapter then repeats this procedure, but with different societies. Underlying this comparative methodology is the idea that from the examination of different cases, chosen because of some marked difference in their characteristic features from those in Britain, a more general conclusion may be drawn about the phenomenon in question. This is the task of the final chapter in each part which also draws progressively on the conclusions of the previous part. The book then turns to the crisis with which it began and seeks to show how these general sociological considerations may be employed for estimating where we are likely to go from here.

PART 1:

Instrument of Collective Bargaining

CHAPTER II

The Sociology of Industrial Relations Systems

The term 'collective bargaining' was introduced by Beatrice Potter to distinguish between 'negotiations through authorized representatives' and 'individual exchange' (Potter, 1891). Later with her husband, she referred to it as one of 'three distinct instruments or levers' which trade unionists employ to enforce their regulations, the others being the methods of mutual insurance and legal enactment. 'In unorganized trades the individual workman, applying for a job, accepts or refuses the terms offered by the employer, without communication with his fellow-workmen, and without any other consideration than the exigencies of his own position. For the sale of his labour he makes, with the employer, a strictly individual bargain. But if a group of workmen concert together and send representatives to conduct the bargaining on behalf of the whole body, the position is at once changed. Instead of the employer making a series of separate contracts with isolated individuals, he meets with a collective will, and settles, in a single agreement, the principles upon which, for the time being, all workmen of a particular group or class or grade, will be engaged.' (S and B. Webb, 1898.) Commenting on this distinction between the individual and the collective bargain, Flanders has pointed out that in the actual practice of industrial relations it is more correct to regard the latter as 'regulating, rather than as replacing' the former. [The individual workman makes his bargain with the employer in the context, so to speak, of collective regulations governing the sale and purchase of labour] The Webbs, indeed, may be faulted for placing too much emphasis on the purely *economic* aspects of industrial relations. It is more accurate to regard collective bargaining as a 'process of negotiation' than to think of it as a market activity. Thus Flanders counters the Webbs' economism with an emphasis on industrial agreements as 'compromise settlements of power conflicts'. The processes involved are not economic so much as political 'in the broadest sense of the word'. (Flanders, 1968.)

At the same time, Flanders manages to avoid going to the other extreme of over-politicizing his analysis. Trade unions, he argues, act in a dual capacity when negotiating collective agreements. On the one hand they are power or pressure groups, using the collective willingness to work, or to refrain from working, as a lever to force an employer to come to terms with them. On the other hand, they work together with employers in the making of 'private' legislation, the rules and orders which control not only wages but conditions of work: 'dismissal, discipline, promotion and training, which cannot by any stretch of the imagination be included under price'. The reason for this, Flanders thinks, arises from the nature of work: 'Labour is more than a commodity because it cannot be isolated from the life of the labourer. For those employees on whose behalf a trade union acts in a collective bargain (who may or may not be members of the union) the effects of its action extend beyond the securing of material gains to the establishment of *rights* in industry; the right to a defined rate of wages, the right not to have to work longer than a certain number of hours, the right to be paid for holidays, and so on.' Collective bargaining, that is to say, is more properly conceived as prescribed by an institutional framework; this framework is informed by what has aptly been called 'industrial jurisprudence'. An industrial relations system is thus an institutionalized system—in the sociological usage of that term—and is amenable to the same kind of analysis which sociologists use for the examination of any institutionalized system whatsoever.

Perhaps the most painstaking attempt to undertake this analysis has been made by Dunlop (1958). Extending the categories of analysis beyond the rules and regulations *per se* to include 'an ideology which binds the industrial relations system together', he argues that such a system at any moment of time is best regarded as 'comprised of certain actors' in certain contexts, so that the rules are seen as 'created to govern the actors at the work place and work community'. This ideology-actor frame of reference Dunlop took from the work of Parsons and Smelser (1956); indeed he asserts specifically, in their manner, that an industrial relations system may be thought of analytically as a 'sub-system' of an industrial society, overlapping but not identical with the economic system, which is more broadly understood and which may also be treated analytically as a sub-system of that society. Dunlop's analysis, it should be emphasized, does not employ the particular categories used by Parsons and Smelser in their work, for all that he sketches out a note on the possibility of so employing those categories in this field. What he does instead is to make use of their type of equilibrium calculus for a scheme of his own, more immediately appealing to labour economists, like himself, who have felt the need for a more elaborate and theoretical analysis than was readily available to them at that time.

The reference in Dunlop's work to 'actors' rather than to 'people' serves to draw attention to the fact that in their *interaction* with others in the system under consideration only certain forms of behaviour are considered appropriate and relevant. Hence the identification of the actors in a system is tantamount to the identification of what sociologists usually refer to as role-players. The buyers and sellers of labour power within a labour market are actors, in the sense that they are 'doers' or 'reagents', to use Dunlop's words. Their approach to each other, that is to say, is influenced by their knowledge of the employment situation, the wages which different employers are prepared to offer and other workers to accept, the kind of skills possessed by those who are already employed and those who are seeking employment. Such knowledge and their personal intentions with respect to work and its rewards determine how they interpret each other's point of view. Once the contract of employment is concluded, however, these 'actors' become role-players—employers and employees—within an enterprise which is part of the industrial relations system; their relationship to each other, while still influenced by the labour market, is now *defined* by the rules of conduct deemed appropriate to employment *per se*. Dunlop, to be sure, identifies not two but three sets of actors in the industrial relations system:

(1) managers 'and their representatives in supervision'

(2) workers (non-managerial) 'and any spokesman'
(3) 'specialized governmental agencies (and specialized private agencies created by the first two actors) concerned with workers, enterprises, and their relationships', or, more precisely in role terms, the representatives of government agencies, employers' associations and trade unions, or their equivalents.

The inclusion of government agencies in this conceptual framework should not be misinterpreted. Where the civil service or state industries are involved in industrial relations systems as employers, the representatives of the government in such a service or in such industries play a managerial role. The agencies referred to by Dunlop, by contrast, are those which intervene in the relationship between managers and workers (or their representatives), either through the execution of laws which govern employment in their society, or through the use of persuasion or coercion to induce the parties to a collective agreement to change that collective agreement in some way, or to conclude a dispute about it in a manner desired by the government of the day. As Dunlop points out, in some industrial relations systems government agencies have powers so great that they can override the other parties on almost all issues. In others their powers are so minor and restricted that it is possible to analyse the system without much reference to them. All industrial societies, however, and indeed all pre-industrial capitalist societies, have some laws governing working arrangements and employment, and some means to enforce these laws. In principle, therefore, the emphasis on the government as a third party to an industrial relations system is not misplaced. What is important is to make allowance for the relative significance of this 'actor' in the system by comparison with the roles played by the others.

Nevertheless, although Dunlop's framework of analysis is acceptable on this point, it is inadequate in other respects. The lack of reference to the owners of industrial property, for example, is surprising. Even a nodding acquaintance with the historical dimension, as outlined in the previous chapter, suggests that the ownership of capital and the lack of it form the dividing line between the classes of employer and employee in capitalist societies and hence represent the focus for disputes, if not for bargaining and negotiation. Why not, then, write the first category of actors in the system as 'owners' rather than as 'managers', and treat the latter as the owners' representatives in supervision? Dunlop is quite clear in his rejection of this alternative. Managers, he writes, 'need have no relationship to the ownership of the capital assets of the workplace'; yet managers possess the power to 'liquidate the enterprise or workplace or change the character of output to be more consonant with the product market or budget'. In an industrial relations system, that is to say, the relevant decisions are made by managers, not owners. To the degree that capitalists are nothing more than shareholders, therefore, they have no direct role in such a system. Of course, as shareholders they have an interest, especially an economic interest, in what goes on inside the factories and workshops owned by the companies in which they have invested capital, just as the wives and children of workers employed by those companies have an interest in the wages their husbands and fathers take home and in the physical and mental health of the wage-earner, particularly as it is affected by the conditions of his work. But, for shareholders, wives, children, there is no admittance to the workplace, except on business. Analytically speaking, ownership as represented by the shareholder, as role-player, is external to an industrial relations system in the same fashion as marriage and parenthood, as represented by the members of a family as role-player, are external to such a system.

To the degree, on the other hand, that capitalists are directors or supervisors of the enterprises they own, they have a direct role in industrial relations. What Dunlop is very conscious of, in fact, is that such a role is not confined to the owners of capital. In some societies government appointees are the alternative to capitalists in the composition of the 'board of directors' of an industrial enterprise. Such appointees, clearly, are not owners in the sense that capitalists are owners. There is no legal definition of their role—which entitles them to a share of the profits—analogous to the provisions of Company Law with its clauses on shareholding and the obligation for directors to be shareholders. Some students of the enterprise in modern society, it is true, have regarded all managers, whether they possess legal rights of possession in business property or not, as 'owners' on the ground that whoever actually *controls* access to raw materials, tools and machines, and finished products of industrial organizations 'for sociological and practical purposes' *in fact* owns them 'whether or not in theory and words' (Burnham, 1964); but this is not Dunlop's point of view. What he seems to imply, indeed, is that the analysis of industrial societies in the days of classical capitalism, that is, before the advent of the joint-stock company, should also clearly differentiate between the ownership and the direction of enterprises, usually the province of the same individual capitalist, and that this analysis should give more weight to the latter than to the former when the relationship between employers and employees is the subject matter. Ownership, from this point of view, is important only to the degree that it determines who shall direct. 'The rise of professional management as contrasted to family management is a relative [sic] new force on emerging nation industrial-relations systems', but management *per se*, in the sense of the making of decisions about the employment of labour and the directing of its operations, has existed ever since journeymen were first employed by master craftsmen to work for them for wages. In this sense it makes no difference today whether the employer is a capitalist or a state nominee. The relationship between him and the employee in their day-to-day conduct at the workplace is hedged about by customs, law, and the rules established by collective negotiations about the right to give instructions and the duty to obey them, the right to claim payment for carrying out those instructions and the duty to make such payments. This is why managers, like workers, are unable to treat the materials, instruments of production, and products of labour, as their own personal property. Such objects belong to the enterprise and not to the role-players within it.

However plausible it may seem, this argument in itself does not justify the sociologist in treating property ownership as altogether irrelevant to an industrial relations system. Indeed, if this argument is not understood completely, it can be taken to imply conclusions which are misleading. Thus Dunlop asserts that employers' associations were 'created' by managers in apparently the same way as trade unions were created by workers. No doubt the former were in some measure a copy of the latter, in the sense that regional and national organizations of employers became permanently established once the trade unions were able to maintain a collective existence also at these levels. Yet to assert that employers' associations were created by managers gives the impression that issues of management *per se* was why the masters responded to the trade unions in this way. Originally the founders were, as a matter of fact, family capitalists and share-owning directors of private companies. Few, if any, were not property owners in this sense. To this day, moreover, the control of employers' associations remains in the hands of directors who make the major decisions about the enterprises they partially own, rather than manage their workers merely. It does not seem reasonable to claim, therefore, that the concern of such directors with their employees is in no way affected by their property interests. In their dealings—as representatives of employers—with trade union leaders as representatives of employees, it is unlikely that dividends on invested capital have no influence on the line they take. Of course, all employers, whether they are property owners or not, are concerned with profitability in the sense that wages and salaries are a cost of production for them and that they seek to end the year with a credit balance; but what is lacking in Dunlop's approach is recognition of the fact that what happens to the profits plays an important part in negotiations *at this level*, and what happens to the profits *is* related to who owns the enterprise.

The first set of actors in Dunlop's scheme must therefore be amended to read: 'directors and their representatives in supervision', in order to remove the misleading impact, on the English reader at least, of the word 'manager'. This amendment, to be sure, does not make room for property ownership as it stands, since the word 'director' merely refers to role-players on boards of control, whether in private or public enterprise, and is thus quite compatible with the notion that control can be separated from *ownership* within the organization. What is needed further, therefore, is an amendment to the three 'sets of givens' which Dunlop considers as 'decisive in shaping the rules established by the actors in any industrial relations system'.

Briefly, these are:

(1) the technical and social characteristics of the workplace

(2)   the market constraints on the enterprise
(3)   the power of the actors in the wider society

To these must now be added:

(4)   the system of property ownership which decides who is to direct operations

All these are variables which, differing from society to society and, within the same society, from industry to industry, stamp a particular impression on the relationship between the role-players, and to a large extent dominate the kinds of rules which they establish to guide their conduct in the workplace. Collective bargaining, it is assumed here, varies according to the pull which all four of these constraints exercise upon the role-players within an industrial relations system.

A further criticism of Dunlop's conception of 'actors' should be noted at this point. To some of his readers his idea of 'system' is of 'an essentially deterministic mechanism'. Although he is 'particularly persuasive in explaining the forces shaping the more substantive aspects of industrial relations', he leaves out of account the extent to which 'key leaders' in enterprises, trade unions, employers' associations and government agencies are able to impose their personalities on the system of relationships in which they are involved (Walton and McKersie, 1965). Dunlop's actors are *not* persons. Even when he admits that each of them 'may be said to have its own ideology', he appears to have in mind a set of ideas and beliefs commonly held by the actors as a *class* of role-players, rather than the individual attitudes of people who are sometimes in accord and sometimes in conflict about what it is right and proper for them personally to demand or to concede in a system, constrained but not determined by the four factors referred to above. No doubt the use of the term 'actor' in this context carries the implication that some degree of self-determination is possible within the system, but Dunlop is neither clear nor precise about when and in what ways people can act to change the rules or to resist the influences which changes in their environment exert upon them.

The history of collective bargaining, it must be confessed, has been largely written in terms of outstanding trade union leaders, businessmen and Ministers of State, whose will power and capacity to move their fellows have been seen as significant. Are we to conclude, therefore, that Dunlop thinks the historians have been at fault in this regard? While it must be admitted that some over-emphasis on personal biographies has entered into their chronicles, it is surely an error of equal magnitude to make no room at all for personality as a variable within the system. At least to the degree that relations between employers and employees are changed as some people leave the system and others join so that the balance of 'dominant personalities, with attributes like authoritarianism and dogmatism' (Blain and Gennard, 1970) is changed, to this degree will a factor intrude which is not covered by the elements in Dunlop's analysis. It is, that is to say, necessary to recognize that industrial relations systems require analysis at the behavioural as well as the institutional level (Margerison, 1969). Even at the workplace, what trade unions attempt to do and succeed in doing are influenced by inter-personal relations between their members as individuals, as well as by the formal, collective designation of the rights and duties of members and shop-stewards *vis-à-vis* supervisors, foremen, managers and full-time officials.

Indeed, if it be admitted that at this level the trade union is an *additional* source of authority over the individual worker, as well as his representative in challenging managerial prerogative (Fox, 1971), how he will behave when faced by a conflicting demand on his loyalties as employee and as union member will depend upon his personal responses to such role conflicts in this and other similar situations. Dunlop's actor-worker must, therefore, be replaced in a strict scheme of role analysis by at least two role-players, the employee and the trade union member— an amendment that has the added advantage of serving to emphasize the ideological nature of the conflict, since workers on the shop floor stand in a subordinate relationship to the representatives in supervision imposed over them by their employers and in an egalitarian relationship to their fellow workers as equal voting members of their union. However much trade unions may have their democratic principles distorted at the national level by the exigencies of large-scale organizations, the authority which they exercise at the workplace is one of the will of many members *vis-à-vis* the will of the few, whereas the authority of management is the will of the few to command the actions of the many, regardless of their wishes in the matter.

This raises the question of whether Dunlop's actor-manager ought also to be amended further to take account of this authority of the trade union at the shop floor level. When a supervisor talks to a shop steward as a representative of his union rather than as an employee in the shop, what kind of behaviour is he constrained to follow? The concept of collective bargaining as a process of negotiation suggests the term 'negotiator', in this context for *both parties*, although the notion of equality which this usage implies should be seen factually to derive from the balance of power between the union and the enterprise at any moment of time rather than from that kind of democratic ideology which holds that all involved should count for one and no more than one. Collective negotiations for the most part entail a hierarchy of negotiator representatives on both sides, supervisor and shop steward, manager and local official, director and national organizer. Disputes which cannot be solved at one level pass up the hierarchy to the next. This procedure is a product of the nature of the hierarchical organization of both trade union and firm-cum-employers' association and the pressure group quality of the former which has won negotiating concessions from the latter. Here again, therefore, whether or not a dispute is solved at this level or passed on for solution elsewhere cannot be predicted without knowledge of the personalities of the individuals making the decisions.

Nevertheless, although the personality factor should not be omitted in studying behaviour in an industrial relations system, its significance should not be misunderstood. Whether or not any individual is successful in making his presence felt depends upon the extent to which he is able to get others to respond to his endeavours. Does he persuade them to interpret the rules and regulations in a manner different from that which they have been accustomed and more in keeping with their purpose as he sees it? Does he, in fact, talk them into changing not only the latent but also the manifest content of these same rules and regulations? Unless there are collective responses of these kinds no individual can influence the system. Hence, the student of industrial relations must recognize that the personality factor must not be treated as if it operated immediately upon the collective bargaining process. Rather must it be seen to work at one remove, so to speak, through the groups who are actually involved in the negotiations. To leave it out of the analysis altogether is to omit an important explanatory variable in the dynamics of the system, but to put it in implies no more than the admission that the views and actions of some individuals have an impact on their fellows. The study of trade unionism, that is to say, does not entail a detailed examination of the psychology of personality types and of the social, psychological and biological factors which produce different personalities at different times and in different places. All that is required is acknowledgment of the fact that some trade unionists and employers make more of an impact on the system than others. It is not necessary to consider why it is they rather than somebody else.

The industrial relations system, thought of as an institutionalized set of interacting role-players, may thus be set out schematically, as follows; the actors have been given fictitious names and the broken lines represent relationships mediated by an unspecified number of intermediate role-players.

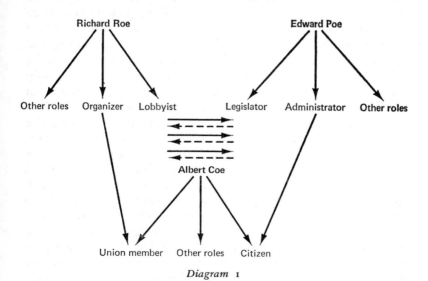

PRESSURE GROUP LOBBYING

Diagram 1

The institutional analysis of industrial relations, condensed to its essentials in this diagram, implies that each of the three sets of inter-role relationships—collective bargaining, enterprise organization and union organization—forms a role system in the sociological sense, for all that each to some degree impinges upon the others. The rules and regulations which prescribe the role behaviour for the role-players in any one set, that is to say, may be seen both logically and factually as distinct from those operating in the other two. The rights and duties of the actors performing roles in that set pertain to those roles *alone* and are not to be confused with those pertaining elsewhere. This does not mean that there is never ambiguity for the actor. Often the role-players in a system are required to act by reference to tacitly understood, customary practices which they would find difficult to clarify if challenged. Even where rules and regulations are clearly set down in print, their interpretation is not always altogether obvious, not only to the observer but also to those who are trying to implement them. Sometimes, too, actors get muddled about what is required of them and attempt to play a role in one system, although the relationships with which other actors think they are faced is that of another.

Nevertheless, the distinction between systems is important, not because it is a commonplace of sociological analysis to draw attention to it, but because the actors themselves see the world in these terms. The very language of collective bargaining and of enterprise and union organization is witness to this fact; for the vocabulary is taken from labels applied to role behaviour in everyday, industrial life by those who get their living, not from analysing it but from working it. Neither sociologists nor other students of industrial relations more generally, invented the words and phrases which are used to refer to these systems, although it is true that they have tried to understand them in their own fashion, using the terminology of their several disciplines. Even the concept of system, which has been especially subjected to criticism by some methodologists because of its use by biologists and physicists in a different context and with different meanings, has been commonly employed by participants in these systems, when describing their intention to organize themselves collectively and to describe those features of the *social* world which have facilitated or hindered their efforts. To assume, therefore, that the reference to social systems must perforce imply a belief in the impotence of human beings is unwarranted. On the contrary, in *this* world men consciously fabricate systems of interlocking roles in order to obtain control over what would otherwise be at best unintelligible and capricious.

Critics of organic and thermodynamic parallels or analogues in the sociological analysis of systems have also occasionally assumed that the use of the term necessarily implies that all systems have the same, basic character of persistence through the harmonious balance of parts. This is, apparently, how organisms and mechanisms maintain themselves in a state of equilibrium in spite of changes in the environment. Clearly, however, this cannot be true of the three systems represented formally in the above diagram. That which links employers and employees in the industrial enterprise, for example, although demonstrating elements of consensus, is fundamentally one of conflict. Although many employers, top managers, politicians and other people outside industry may have a vision of it which approximates to the professional football team, united in its determination to win goals for the side (Fox, 1966) their consistent tendency in the practice of their daily business affairs has been to act as though they saw it very differently. Employees in effect are regarded as a means merely to their employers' purposes. Whether or not they are employed at all is a decision which is not theirs to make, but the prerogative of those who direct the organization. From this point of view, wages and salaries paid to employees are a cost, not to be considered unless some advantage to the payer accrues from the payment, and therefore a charge to be set against the employer's assessments of the possibility of gain to the enterprise and income to himself. At its crudest, that is to say, the more there is for one role-player in this relationship, the less there is for the other, no matter how large the eventual product of their combined efforts. To the degree that the system of interlocking *roles* persists, it is because the actors do not press their claims to the limit, but this willingness to compromise should not be misinterpreted so to obscure the essential lack of agreement about aims and intentions and economic interest.

On the other hand, the system which links trade union organizers to the union members, although subject to dissension, is primarily one of common agreement. The full-time officials of trade unions, to be sure, are employees of their trade unions and hence experience conflicts of interest with the elected, executive committee members over their salaries as officials, but this is not the role relationship at issue here. Insofar as union leaders and union members are linked together organizationally for the purpose of collective action *on behalf of the members as such*, the analogy of the football team applies. Undoubtedly there will be occasions for personal disagreement about the appropriate means to use for this end. Some members may be preoccupied with their sectional interests to the disadvantage of others; some union organizers may use the members as a means merely for their personal ambition; but the recognition that trade unions rest not upon a cash but a voting nexus between participants, where each vote including that of the leader counts for no more than one, is an admission that the more for one, less for the other form of reciprocity, typical of employment, does not apply in this case. In brief, the two systems—enterprise relationships between employers and employees, trade union relationships between organizers and members—are marked by so radically different features that to use the term 'equilibrium' or 'homeostasis' in the biological or thermodynamic sense, without appropriate qualification, is likely to be misleading. A social system persists in equilibrium because the majority of people involved in playing its roles see no purpose in changing it or no satisfactory way of changing it immediately even if they wish to, and also because human beings are quite capable of maintaining relations of conflict in some parts of their everyday lives while co-operating in others.

The difference between the two systems linked by collective bargaining explains why it is so often puzzling to the observer. Essentially, of course, bargaining itself is based on consensus. Unless there is willingness to negotiate there can be no negotiation. Neither party to the process of bargaining, indeed, intends to alter fundamentally the relationships which operate within the systems which it links. Trade unionists as a general rule do not set out to abolish the employer-employee connection, although they may take steps to change aspects of its environment, such as property ownership, which they think bear harshly on the employee. The concept of workers' democracy used in this context does not usually mean that the members of boards of directors should be directly elected by and from the workers, with each member having one vote, in parallel with the practice of electing trade union executives. Rather does it mean the recognition of the trade union as a kind of permanent opposition with representatives not only on the Board but on various committees at different levels of the organization which *employs* its members as workers (Coates, 1968). Similarly, employers do not seek to abolish the organizer-member relationship in trade unions.

Although they were slow to recognize the right of trade unionists to bargain with them and to this day some, no doubt, would prefer an industrial world in which trade unions did not exist, there is no evidence of general, concerted action on their part to change this wish into reality. For all that they often express the view that trade union leaders should have more power than they apparently possess to discipline those of their members who fail to honour collective agreements, they nevertheless seem to see this as a case of strengthening the rule of the majority over a recalcitrant minority. They do not want trade unions to be converted formally into oligarchies through the senior members being accorded more votes per head than the rank-and-file. Collective bargaining, in other words, relates two systems which individually select the representatives for negotiation on very different principles. Hence the relationship between the negotiators as such cannot be inferred simply from the other roles they play in the industrial enterprise or in the trade union. If the latter, therefore, may be legitimately likened to a football team, collective bargaining may be likened to a football match. The rules of the game have been developed to govern how the members of the different teams are to behave with respect to each other, and these rules cannot be inferred from the way in which the members behave towards members of their own sides.

In the chapters which follow all these features of the systems analysis of industrial relations are taken for granted. Obviously, it is beyond the scope of a book of this length to demonstrate in detail how such systems analysis may be applied to contemporary collective bargaining, especially if this is carried out comparatively over more than one country. Sociologists, however, believe comparative studies to be illuminating, largely because of the way in which they reveal differences between systems which in many other respects are similar, and similarities in systems which otherwise are different, and hence bring out the significant aspects of the phenomenon in question. The procedure followed here, therefore, has been to select a topic which is the concern of current discussion in this country but which nevertheless exemplifies issues of more general, sociological importance, and, in the subsequent chapter, to examine the same issue in a very different context. This means that many other aspects of contemporary trade unionism are ignored; but it is hoped that the examination of a single issue in this way will demonstrate the sociological contribution to our understanding of events, and that the reader will thereby be enabled to apply other features of systems analysis to whatever aspects of industrial relations in this country interest him.

CHAPTER III

Collective Bargaining in Britain

For some time now the British shop steward has been regularly seen as playing a 'vital role ... in negotiations with management over terms and conditions of employment', as an official view has expressed it. This role has indeed been seen as so vital that the First Secretary of State and Secretary for Employment and Productivity under the Labour government instructed the Commission on Industrial Relations in November, 1969, to examine and report on the facilities which shop stewards and 'other equivalent workplace representatives of trade union members' should have for carrying out these negotiations in a satisfactory manner (Commission on Industrial Relations, 1971). This instruction followed upon an earlier policy statement which had held that workplace relationships were crucial to Britain's economic future but were, at the same time, suffering from serious defects. 'In practice an increasing amount of bargaining, and an increasing proportion of the wage packet, is settled outside the "formal system" by informal understandings and arrangements between shop stewards and managers or foremen at workplace level. Yet this concentration on "informality", and the network of shop floor arrangements and understandings that result from it, create serious problems. Few clear principles and standards are developed to settle shop floor grievances.' (*In Place of Strife*, 1969.)

Accordingly, employers were urged to negotiate 'formal, comprehensive and authoritative company or factory agreements' to 'cover the numbers and constituencies of shop stewards: provide for facilities for them to consult their members and to negotiate with management'. The inspiration for these proposals seems to have come from the Report of the Royal Commission on Trade Unions and Employers' Associations which had had two research papers prepared on shop stewards (McCarthy, 1967, and McCarthy and Parker, 1968) and which had made known its own view that unofficial strikes in Britain would persist 'so long as neither employers nor trade unions are willing adequately to recognize, define and control the part played by shop stewards in our collective bargaining system' (Donovan, 1968). As opposed to the analysis proferred in the previous chapter, that is to say, the commonly held view in Britain at this time was that negotiations by shop stewards were somehow at variance with the requirements of a properly constituted system of industrial relations.

The Royal Commission, in particular, emphasized that in many trade union rule-books shop stewards 'or their counterparts are mentioned only because the union relies upon them to collect subscriptions. The representative functions of stewards are referred to with a surprising infrequency. The rules of the Transport and General Workers' Union and of the Union of Shop, Distributive and Allied Workers, for example, say nothing about such functions. The rules of the Amalgamated Engineering Union leave it to the District Committees to define the powers of shop stewards with the Executive Council's approval "subject to national agreements". Very few unions make any attempt, in their rules, to provide for the calling of shop floor meetings or seek to prescribe their constitutional powers. The practice of issuing shop stewards' handbooks is no more than a partial remedy for this reticence in the rules.' Such an emphasis on the formality of the written word fitted very neatly into the Royal Commission's contention that there were in fact not *one* but *two* systems of collective bargaining operating side by side in Britain —'the one is the formal system embodied in the official institutions. The other is the informal system created by the actual behaviour of trade unions and employers' associations, of managers, shop stewards and workers.' The meaning of this is not clear, because if the informal system is the one actually in use, it is difficult to envisage what the concept of a formal system embodied in the official institutions is supposed to refer to. Nevertheless the implication of all this concentration on the role of the shop steward is plain. He is not to be thought of as an official negotiator in the institutional sense. In the light of the contrary assertion in the previous chapter it is relevant to ask here therefore: who is?

The Royal Commission was strangely silent on this point, although an analysis of rule-books, carried out earlier, might have been consulted to illuminate the question further. Within the administrative system of the trade union the key local unit is the branch, and the trade union officer who is 'in the centre of affairs, directing, organizing and administering the work of the branch' is the branch secretary, one of whose many functions is that of negotiating (Roberts, 1956). It is true that the time a secretary spends on average in negotiation is much less than he spends on his other duties (Clegg, Killick and Adams, 1961), but this merely serves to underline one point made in the previous chapter that, although the organization of a trade union is a separate system from that of collective bargaining, some individuals will perform roles in both systems. Indeed, one possible explanation for the rise in importance of the shop steward as negotiator is to be sought in the changing nature of the *branch* secretary's role *within the union* and its relationship therefore with his 'assistants', the *shop* stewards. The Royal Commission failed to report on this, although one interpretation of its position is that it believed the latter to have usurped the negotiating function of the former. An alternative way of looking at the issue is to consider whether, as trade unions grow in size and their business affairs become more complex, tasks which were formerly carried out by a single role-player become the separate responsibilities of two. Trade union rule-books specify the recruitment of members, the collection of subscriptions and the reporting of malpractices and grievances to the branch, as functions of shop stewards (Roberts, 1956) because these were the tasks which branch secretaries found they were unable to do satisfactorily. Once branch membership grew in size through the enrolment of an increasing proportion of eligible workers in a growing number of 'shops', employing a larger labour force, branch secretaries were obliged to find other union members to carry out these tasks in the shops for them.

Three sets of statistics illustrate the trends:

(1) Between 1920 and 1968, although the number of trade unions in the United Kingdom fell from 1,384 to 534, the

total membership rose from 8,350,000 to 10,050,000 (Department of Employment and Productivity, 1971). Through amalgamations and other events trade unions grew in size.

(2) Over roughly the same period the proportion of eligible workers who were also trade union members increased from 37.6% (1921) to 42.6% (1946), although with considerable variations between industries (Bain, 1967). As these figures indicate, trade unions are still far from complete. The 100% shop is indeed very rare (McCarthy, 1964). Nevertheless, trade union recruitment has been increasingly successful.

(3) Between 1930 and 1963 the number of establishments employing at least 1,000 workers, rose from 535 to 1,189, while the number employing less than 1,000 fell from 201,690 to 83,037 (figures calculated from Table 206 of Department of Employment and Productivity, 1971). Apparently more workers in the same occupation, eligible for membership in the same unions, were employed in the same shops.

The stewards in such shops are responsible for recruitment and subscriptions and are expected to listen to grievances. The branch secretary is necessarily more remote, unless by chance he happens to work in a member's shop. Of course, one way in which trade unions have been reorganized to cope with this problem has been to establish workplace branches rather than branches based on members' residence. Thus 26% of the shop stewards covered in the Royal Commission's survey said that all their branch members were from their own workplace (McCarthy and Parker, 1968), but this change has not affected the other major role problem, that the branch secretary, whether he is in a member's workplace or not, has still a multitude of other tasks to perform by virtue of his office in the union hierarchy, while the shop steward's duties are relatively few.

In Britain, too, there is another reason for the shop steward taking over increasingly the role of negotiator. In one study a large majority of personnel officers (Clegg, Killick and Adams, 1961) and, in another, a similarly large majority of personnel officers *and* works managers (McCarthy and Parker, 1968) said that they preferred to negotiate with the shop stewards in their factories rather than with the full-time union officers. The 'lay' worker, they thought, was more likely to have 'intimate knowledge of the circumstances of the case'. At the same time union officers have, for the most part, expressed satisfaction with their respective roles *vis-à-vis* one another in local negotiations, and local negotiations have become increasingly commonplace in British industry. Thus, whereas before the war industry-wide bargaining was the norm, the post-war trend has been for 'centrally negotiated agreements to leave considerable scope for local adjustments' (Ministry of Labour, 1960) and the task of making such adjustments on the union side has been carried out by shop stewards familiar with local customs and expectations. By the time that the Royal Commission issued its Report in 1968, workplace bargaining had come to be accepted as the chief characteristic of the British system. This is why the role of shop steward has come to be seen as of crucial significance.

To understand collective bargaining in Britain, therefore, it is necessary to appreciate the nature of the transition from a system of wage determination by Joint Industrial Councils to one of considerable autonomy in wage negotiations by the managers in individual companies and the shop stewards on the company's payroll. Throughout the later decades of the nineteenth century and right up to the end of the Second World War, if not until 1960, a system had gradually been built up which presupposed that the major issues with which trade unions were concerned could best be settled at a national level through meetings of the representatives of trade union executive committees with representatives of employers' federations. Breakdowns at this level did occur, of course, and where they were not solved by conciliation or arbitration, were followed by a strike or a lockout which provoked a strike. All such strikes, it should be noted, were official; they were called by the trade union executive who would authorize payment of money to the strikers from the appropriate union funds—in marked contrast to the more recent events where the great bulk of strikes have been unofficial (Donovan, 1968), even though union executives seem to have been prepared to pay dispute benefit after the event.

The British government had played a major part in the development of this centralized system; for although some industries had established nationally-based negotiating machinery in the nineteenth century on their own initiative, the chief

impetus for growth after the First World War was the establishment of Whitley Councils for Civil Servants and other government employees, and the injunction to the Ministry of Labour
to promote Joint Industrial Councils in all sections of industry. The Trade Boards and Wages Councils Acts, from 1909
to 1959, are especially revealing of the official attitude in this
respect. They empowered the Minister to establish machinery
for wage regulation in industries where adequate arrangements
between employers' federations and trade unions did not exist.
Such regulation, it was understood, would continue only for so
long as such arrangements continued to be wanting and would
cease once organizations in an industry could recommend to
the Minister that a Joint Industrial Council was possible. This
meant that the first objective of any Wages Council was to com-
mit suicide (Wedderburn, 1965). This general preference for
voluntary collective bargaining without state regulation, maintained by successive governments irrespective of their political
objectives and by generations of the administrators serving
them, is extremely well illustrated in the Ministry of Labour's
Handbook, produced originally for use by its staff in 1945 and
revised in 1953 and 1961. Throughout, its authors presuppose
that local negotiation merely supplements an adequate industry-
wide system and regard the shop steward as little more than a
link between the members of a trade union working in a shop
and the full-time officials of the union.

How, then, did local bargaining come to preponderate in the
British system? One possibility was heavily emphasized by the
Royal Commission—'the pressure of full employment which has
been almost continuous since 1938. Full employment encourages
bargaining about pay at the factory and workshop levels. Because they cannot easily be replaced the bargaining power of
individual groups of workers is increased; and because their employer is anxious to keep them and perhaps to recruit new
workers, he may be willing to "bid up" their pay without much
prompting' (Donovan, 1968). Even the nationalized industries,
which are monopolies and hence completely unified on the employers' side, have been influenced by the long period of full
employment, although in their case the adjustments have
usually occurred in the form of local arrangements about incentives and overtime working. Unofficial strikes and the rise to

importance of the role of shop steward may thus be seen as symptoms of the power of the work group in circumstances where individual workers have the alternatives of absenteeism and job turnover if local managers should take too intransigent a line on a wage dispute, and where competition between employers for local labour has emphasized worker shortages and hence made negotiation at this level more likely. The marked rise in the status of personnel officers (Roberts and Gennard, 1970) makes sense in this context, not because a distinct managerial role has been deliberately forged for workplace bargaining but because of the locally felt need for a specialist officer to pursue 'satisfactory human relations' within the factory. The purpose of such an officer is to concern himself with forms of recruitment, training and 'welfare' for the mainly manual personnel, so that improvements may accrue in the performance of individual employees while they are at work on the one hand, and in the general stability of the total labour force on the other.

Thus full employment, although possibly the chief factor in the emergence to significance of the shop steward's role, is not the sole factor in operation. Another of Dunlop's environmental factors—the technical and social characteristics of the workplace—has also been influential. In very general terms the trend in technological advance in most industries is in the direction of a progressive increase in the capital-labour ratio; more expensive and elaborate machines per worker. This has made continuity of output more crucial to the calculation of profit possibilities than the cost of wages as such, and the need for technical efficiency in the men who operate the machines and organizational ability in the men who manage them has focussed the employer's attention on the quality of personnel. At the same time the growth in the size of his establishments and the concommitant increase in the number of levels of supervisory management has complicated the process of communication up, down, and across the hierachies of his production units.

That such workplace issues have become significant is indicated by the statistics of unofficial strikes. According to the Ministry of Labour (Donovan, 1968) about 30% of them are about 'working arrangements, rules and discipline' and a further 15% about 'redundancy, dismissals, suspension, etc.'—'causes' which probably also relate to worker-manager frictions on the shop floor. This total of about 45% compares with just under 50% for 'wages' as such. Thus, even if unemployment continues to rise in the country, as it has since 1968, and eventually reaches a level comparable to that of the inter-war period, it is unlikely that there will be a reversal to the type of nation-wide bargaining of those times. Although official strikes on a national basis have recently been occurring there still remain many issues of dispute on the shop floor for which the union steward continues to be the crucial figure. Indeed, the emphasis in the Report of the Commission on Industrial Relations on facilities which should be made available to shop stewards (Commission on Industrial Relations, 1971) directs attention *inter alia* towards their gaining increasing responsibility for consultation and communication. The sociological interpretation of these events leads to the conclusion that the role of the steward is steadily broadening from that of workplace negotiator merely to that of link man, not so much between the rank-and-file union member and the officials in his union (although that is also true) but rather between the rank-and-file employee and the management of his firm. Indeed, this trend is already beginning to raise new problems for employers in the sense that first-line supervisors complain of feeling excluded from information which is readily available to shop stewards.

So far the emphasis here has largely been laid on features of the enterprise organization which have led to changes in the role of the steward in the system of collective bargaining. This, of course, is consonant with the discussion in the previous chapter about the way in which external systems of role relationships have been said to impinge upon this system. It is now relevant to ask whether there are features of the manner of union organization in Britain, which have also influenced the shop steward's role, other than the growth in the number of union members at the steward's place of work. Some observers, for example, have pointed to the part played in workplace negotiation by the fact that in many British enterprises employees are organized, not by one union but by many. Such multi-unionism does not seem to have been of much significance when national negotiation was the norm. Some kind of loose coordination between union executives was all that was necessary to prevent negotiations from over-favouring the claims of any one union. Workplace bargaining, however, has brought to prominence considerations of differentials between occupations, which were there before but not emphasized. 'Shop stewards of different unions have to be brought together to compare wages and conditions in their respective constituencies within the plant, to formulate joint policies on workshop issues, and to make common agreements with their employers. It is this combination of stewards from different unions that give the workplace representative system such a large degree of autonomy from the unions proper.' The establishment of Joint Shop Stewards Committees and the emergence of a new role within the system—that of the chief steward, senior steward, or convenor—who not only brings together in the enterprise the stewards from his own union but also consults with those from other unions—justifies the argument that the 'workplace representative system is now an elaborate institution in its own right' (Turner, Clack and Roberts, 1967). Indeed, a striking example of this formalization of the negotiating role in the workplace is that within the car industry a new type of strike has been identified—the unofficial-unofficial strike—one that is approved neither by the union officially nor, initially at least, by the leaders of the shop stewards in the plant. Recognition of this possibility makes it plain that the Royal Commission's contrast between nation-wide bargaining as the formal system and workplace bargaining as the informal is more misleading than enlightening. Both have a measure of formality and informality in their make-up.

The institutionalization of workplace bargaining, in other words, comprises *inter alia* a set of recognized rules and regulations about the role of the shop steward in the workplace which, in the British context, often constitutes a system of its own, a set of role relationships for stewards from different unions and for the convening and governance of meetings of shop stewards in the workplace. Whether this system would have come about if there had not also been full employment over a generation and if those changes in the organization of industry, described above, had not taken place, it is legitimate to question. Nevertheless, the particular form which workplace organization has for the most part taken in Britain has been coloured by the multi-unionism prevailing in British industry. This implies, of course, that where all the workers in an enterprise are members of the same union, institutionalization on the shop floor will not have this degree of elaborateness. It also implies that even in this country a simpler shop floor system of collective bargaining, with perhaps rather more informality, is likely to be found wherever some approximation to a single industry union prevails. Examples of such a system occur in the National Union of Boot and Shoe Operatives or even, some people say, in the National Union of Mineworkers. On the other hand, since in this last case the negotiating procedure was laid down when the industry was nationalized in 1947, the rights and duties of each role-player at each level has been set out formally in writing (Marsh and McCarthy, 1968), as is usual when legislation prescribes procedure. Thus, the generalized treatment of the focal role of shop steward in this chapter requires amendment when applied to concrete instances; allowance must be made for whether an industry is nationalized or not, is multi-union or not, is large-scale or not, is capital intensive or not; and it is relevant to ask whether a more homogeneous system of collective bargaining might reveal rather different practices. The next chapter is devoted to an examination of this question.

CHAPTER IV

Collective Bargaining
under Communism

Trade Unions in Communist societies are for the most part industrial-enterprise unions. They are organized on the principle that *all* those employed in an enterprise, whether as managerial, technical, clerical or manual workers, are eligible for membership of the single trade union which is responsible for the workers in the industry of which the enterprise is part. Since this means that the individual who is responsible to the state for the conduct of the enterprise—the director—is a member of the same trade union as his subordinates, it is difficult to envisage at first glance how there can be room for collective bargaining between them. Indeed, it is a commonplace of Western commentary on trade unionism in such societies to allege that although there are organizations which are called trade unions within them, these are not trade unions in the accepted sense of the term; they merely serve the interests of the government and act as an alternative means for communicating government policies to the workers; they exhort them to higher productivity and hence supplement the directors' efforts in the same direction.

On the other hand, since this industrial-enterprise, employment union principle of organization has been characteristic of Communist societies since the Russian revolution, it is reasonable to ask, if the trade unions are instruments of government policy, why the Webbs were able to conclude from their visit to Russia in 1932 that 'far from there being less collective bargaining in the U.S.S.R. than in Great Britain or the United States, or in Germany before the Hitlerite dictatorship, there is actually very much more than in any country in the world' (S. & B. Webb, 1935). Of course, it is easy to interpret their study of

Soviet Communism as a kind of enormous, propagandist pamphlet, justifying their own *Constitution of a Socialist Commonwealth* as a practical possibility, and therefore to dismiss their view as biased by their readiness to accept as true everything they were told. Yet a generation later a Mission from the International Labour Office reported that 'the omnipresence of Soviet trade unions cannot fail to strike any visitor who has had an opportunity to go a little off the beaten track and to get briefly into touch with industrial and agricultural enterprises' (International Labour Office, 1960b), and confirmed by implication the Webbs' view that trade unions in Russia perform so many functions that it is easy for the foreign student to underestimate their significance in collective bargaining.

The Webbs, it was pointed out above, can be faulted in their analysis of industrial relations generally for placing too much emphasis on bargaining in the context of collective regulations governing the sale and purchase of labour. Hence it is not to be expected that they would attempt to interpret the Russian system in terms of power conflicts. Nevertheless, within the limitations of their approach, it was quite legitimate for them to conclude that the Communist system had resulted in an increase, rather than a decline, of haggling between trade union representatives and the managements of the particular factories in which their members were working. As they saw them, Russian trade unions had been accorded a share in the organization of industry far beyond that accorded to their counterparts in other societies. 'The foreign observer is surprised to find the safety and amenity of places of work, the provision of hospital and sanatorium beds, the measures taken for the prevention of accidents, the provision of additional or better dwelling accommodation for the persons employed, the establishment of crèches and kindergartens for the young children; the workmen's clubhouse and the technical classes provided to enable them to improve their qualifications—and many other matters of importance to the workmen's daily life, dealt with in the detailed agreement drawn up annually in March between the management and the various workmen's committees, in time to allow the management to provide, in the budget for the factory operations, the necessary increases in factory expenditure, which have all to find their place in the General Plan.' If, therefore, there appears to be rather more consensus between managers and trade unionists over potentially disruptive issues, such as output and productivity, than commonly prevails in non-Communist societies, it is possibly because they are in basic agreement over the need to increase the collective product. Bargaining must reasonably begin, it might be thought, where this consensus ends, on the manner of disposing of the surplus of output over input. However, even the Webbs saw that there was more to the situation than this. 'There is,' they wrote, 'the inevitable stream of complaints from individual workmen about real or imaginary ill-treatment, expressing discontent with the piecework rates for their particular jobs, or appealing against dismissal or other disciplinary action.' What they failed to see, inescapably because of their more general approach, was that such complaints might possibly be interpreted as indicative of conflicts arising from the divergent roles which are played in the Russian industrial system.

Consider, for example, the manner in which wages are determined. Both at the time of the Webbs and throughout the history of the U.S.S.R wage scales and wage rates, as opposed to actual earnings, have been decided centrally. The government's planning authorities prepare budgets which estimate the target outputs for a given period and the necessary expenditure for the whole society. The latter includes the pay of political administrators, teachers, doctors, etc. which is prescribed in detail through the Ministry of Finance, and a wages fund for workers in industry and agriculture, which is apportioned to each productive unit to administer. From time to time the actual procedures adopted for such budgeting have varied according to the organization of economic life by the state, whether it was by a People's Commissarist for Labour (until 1934), an Economic Council (until 1940), a Council of Ministers (until 1956), or a State Committee on Labour and Wages (since 1956) which the government held responsible for wage questions. Nevertheless, the general principle has always been the same. The wages fund has been subdivided to take account of the 'quality' of the work done. All workers, that is to say, are divided into grades; the wage rates for each grade are settled on the basis of differential co-efficients, so that at any moment of time there is a fixed ratio of wage rates from the highest to the lowest. Every now and again the differential co-efficients and the wage rates are changed, to narrow or to broaden the nominal wage structure (Nove, 1965), and apparently the All-union Central Council of Trade Unions is involved in this with whatever government agency makes the change, although it is not known publicly how much influence the unions have at this level (Brown, 1966). The point of importance, however, is not union participation at this stage but at the stage of the subsequent conversion of wage rates into earning; for it has been a consistent feature of the Bolshevik system of wage determination that workers may exceed the target output by their combined or individual efforts, and, indeed, may be given incentives to do so, in the form of bonuses and piece-rates which entitle them to extra wages for output above the norm.

The crucial concept for understanding the Russian system of industrial relations, therefore, is the output norm, the estimate of the average of output in a given period of time. At the factory level the primary concern of the trade union is with such norms in the sense that the assignment of workers to work grades, the application of wage rates to specific jobs, and the revision of existing norms is carried out by management and union representatives in consultation. The salaries of engineering-technical (managerial) personnel, it should be understood, are not subject to such union influence, although they also may be inflated by bonuses for factory output in excess of the enterprise target. Obviously a worker can raise his earning either by overfulfilling the norm—producing more units than the output norm for the job—or by getting the enterprise to lower the norm, through his union representatives arguing a successful case for a higher piece-payment per unit. The former does not involve a dispute with management, the latter may. To some extent both managers and workers have a personal interest in keeping norms low since both will benefit from easily overfulfilled norms that have been accepted as reasonable by higher bodies; but in a modern, highly complex and always changing production system a worker's actual job is unlikely to remain the same for long—and certainly rarely for as long as a year at a time—so that the opportunity for disputes occurs quite frequently. For example, where work on one type of material is paid more highly than work on another and the materials are not easily identified, changes in production have led to disputes (Brown, 1966). Where a decline in the efficiency of a machine makes fulfilment of the norm more difficult, workers have similarly been in dispute with their management (McAuley, 1969). In any case, an element of incentive for managers consists in the making of economies in the use of the wages fund, leading them to seek ways of getting more effort from their workers by cutting down on what they see as waste of materials and time. Thus, although directors and workers may be in basic agreement to increase the collective product, since both will receive bonuses in consequence, their relative positions in the system implies that the way in which such increases may be brought about creates friction between them. Certainly McAuley's analysis of disputes between 1957 and 1965 demonstrates that there were many instances of such frictions over wages and hours of work during that period. As she summarized the situation, 'management attempts to stretch the wage fund, the desire to retain or improve on existing levels of managerial earnings, to interpret rulings to benefit production and to dismiss unprofitable employees came into conflict with the union desire to maintain existing levels of earnings or length of holidays, and to safeguard employees' jobs'. (McAuley, 1969.)

Of course, the particular emphasis on collective effort in the Russian system gives it institutional forms of worker-management relations which are quite distinct from the interpretation of such relations in, say, Britain. Co-operation in production means that local trade unions are expected not only to be involved in the planning processes of their enterprises but also to encourage their members fully to participate in production conferences for the discussion of problems involved in the fulfilment of the works' plan. The Russian 'equivalent' of the English shop steward, the trade union group organizer, thus has a much wider set of functions to perform. He 'brings new workers into membership, collects union dues'—much in the manner of shop stewards everywhere—but he also 'has responsibilities for production, protection of workers' rights, and educational and cultural activities' (Brown, 1966). Shop meetings and shop committees are a commonplace of the organization of the factory in this system, and the effect apparently is to implement that kind of human relations policy in industry which the employment of specialist personnel officers outside the Communist system has been intended to achieve. This does not necessarily mean that the consequence is an identity of attitudes towards the place of work and its productive functions on the part of workers and managers. Kolaja's study of a textile factory in Lodz indicates that, if this experience were as typical of Russian as of Polish factory organization, workers perceive their situation strictly in individualistic terms, by contrast to the emphasis by factory directors on the collective goal of production. The workers he talked to were not altogether unsuspicious of management and they seemed to lack the incentive to acquire necessary information about the way the system of production is organized and their part in it (Kolaja, 1960). Indeed, the awareness that even where industrial property is communally owned there can be a conflict of attitudes between workers and managers has given the Jugoslavian organization of Workers' Councils its special impetus, with the conclusion that although functional differentiation continues to exist the hostility to management is less than in the Polish case (Kolaja, 1965).

The place of trade unions in Jugoslavia, therefore, is of particular interest in an examination of collective bargaining under Communism. The emphasis in that country since 1963 has, of course, been on the Councils rather than the trade unions, largely because the Workers' Councils have the power to hire and fire factory directors, a power the unions lack; yet even more important in the present context is the fact that the Councils have the responsibility for establishing the wage scales that apply within the plant. It is true that this is achieved by agreement between the Council, the trade union, and the local municipal authority (or district council if the factory is in a rural area) but it also means that the worker with a grievance has an 'almost embarrassing wealth of grievance procedures available to him: the workers' council, the managing board, the director, the union, the Communist Party'. In consequence, 'the union is hardly ever mentioned by anyone in connection with grievance handling' (Sturmthal, 1964). The work of the Workers' Council may thus be said both to overlap and to compete with that of the trade union, and it is possible therefore that the trade union representative in the shop has become of less significance to his fellow workers than the elected representative to the

Council. On the other hand, evidence of dissatisfaction with the methods of income distribution, and with income levels and differentials, indicates that workers see members of Workers' Councils as managers, taking a managerial point of view when making decisions (Riddell, 1968). This, together with the opinions of a Jugoslavian observer that 'the structure of power in our enterprises is still *very authoritarian*, that the directors and the representatives of the specialized services play first fiddle' (Supek, 1970), suggests the possibility that in time the trade union representative will emerge again as an important role-player in the enterprise.

Writing much earlier about those distinctive characteristics of the Jugoslavian industrial relations system which have made it unique, Dunlop stressed 'the combination of the system of ideology with the problems of rapid industrialization in a relatively underdeveloped country'. The former is, of course, that 'body of common ideas that defines the role and place of each actor and that defines the ideas which each actor holds toward the place and function of the others in the system' (Dunlop, 1958). In the Jugoslavian case this ideology is highly formalized. Less of what each 'actor' has to do in the workplace is left to custom and practice than in countries with a long industrial tradition, although as the Jugoslavians themselves point out there is a discrepancy between what is set down in the rule books and what is carried out in fact. For example, in spite of formal attempts to recruit representatives to the Workers' Council proportionately from all sections of the labour force, there is evidence that the elected members tend to be male and skilled, or highly skilled, workers (Blumberg, 1968). As in all Communist societies, the abolition of private property in industrial production as a means of creating the classless society has faced the draughtsmen of the Jugoslavian constitution with the problem of how best to define the responsibilities of all in industry with respect to one another when the property relationships which have previously decided who directed operations become collectivized. In justifying their experiment the Jugoslavians asserted that the Russian decision to replace private ownership by state ownership had resulted in agencies of the state making the major decisions about what is to be done, who is to do it and what they are to be paid, even at the factory level. The director of an enterprise, from this point of view, is a state nominee responsible to higher political and administrative authorities.

The aim of the Jugoslavians, accordingly, was to confine the responsibilities of government agencies to fiscal and monetary functions at the national level and hence to replace state ownership by community ownership. Thus the technical director of a Jugoslavian enterprise who before 1953 was 'a state official appointed and dismissed by his supervisors, working under their orders, and answerable to them alone for his actions' (International Labour Office, 1963), now became appointed by a committee of representatives from the Workers' Council of the enterprise he was to direct and representatives of the People's Committee of the commune in which it was located. After 1963 this dual system was replaced by appointment by representatives from the Workers' Council. The Jugoslavian industrial system may, therefore, now be said to entail the notion that the workers collectively *own* the factory, although as with all property systems ownership is constrained by legal considerations which, in this instance, prevent them from disposing of the property as they think fit and holds them responsible as trustees to the community, regarded as the ultimate source of authority. In this sense the ideology to which Dunlop referred is unique, but since it is coupled with another with respect to productivity, namely that Jugoslavia must be industrialized rapidly, the appointment of a director is hedged about by enterprise rules on his qualifications and experience which entail that he be better educated than the rank-and-file workers and much more accustomed to giving orders. It is not surprising to learn in consequence that in a personal communication, Kozomara, a Bosnian sociologist who has conducted research in Jugoslavian factories, reported to Riddell that in spite of the Workers' Councils 'an "us-them" feeling exists between workers and management authorities, paralleling the attitudes which have been so frequently found by sociologists in capitalist countries' (Riddell, 1968).

All this serves to draw attention to the issue with which this book began, namely, the distinction between the historically general and the historically specific views of trade unionism. Emphasis on the overriding significance of property ownership implies that collective bargaining should be interpreted differently when the system is defined as collectivist as contrasted with capitalist, when industrial property is publicly owned as compared with privately owned. In the former case all the workers in the enterprise are members of the same trade union, much as all the workers in the same trade were members of the same medieval guild; whereas in the latter the membership of a union is confined to the class of lifelong wage servants and the class of entrepreneurs is excluded. This distinction makes it possible to conceive of collective bargaining under capitalism as the institutionalization of class conflict, since the relationship between the classes in the market for labour and the determination of wages is based on the principle that the capitalist employs workers for his own purposes, not theirs. The concept of the Workers' Council, by contrast, implies that collective bargaining *of this sort* is no longer possible. There are no classes in the capitalist sense; if conflicts remain they will be between the enterprise and other enterprises, between the enterprise and the local commune or the state authorities. The trade union in this system is like the guild also in that it undertakes many welfare activities which are not the responsibility of trade unions in capitalist societies. Yet too many parallels between the guild system and that of the Workers' Councils must be avoided. The tools of the trade and the raw materials worked on by the medieval artisan were individually owned and, until the system began to break down, each apprentice could be confident that one day he would become a master in his own right. The Workers' Council system implies a very different type of industrial property ownership where rights over tools and materials are collectively determined, and although in Jugoslavia serious attempts have been made to get workers to play their part in elections and to consider standing themselves for office, there is very little expectation that more than a tiny fraction of them will ever become a director.

In the previous chapter it was pointed out that the role of the shop steward in British industry has been steadily broadened from that of work-place negotiator merely to one of acting as link man between the rank-and-file employee and the managers of the firm. In the Jugoslavian system this role seems to be played by the Workers' Council representative. Research carried out on the work of the Councils has shown that they were more intensively active when the system was first introduced into the factories than they have been since, largely because the problems which were acute at the beginning were apparently inter-personal, whereas once procedures were developed to deal with these, the problems of the economic policy of the enterprise, its relation to markets and with other enterprises, have been left in the main to the director and other experts to decide. Now the participation of workers increases only when direct personal interests are involved, as in 'the division of profit or a rise in wages, the distribution or building of flats, the organization of transport from and to work' (Supek, 1970)—issues remarkably like those which seem to cause an increase in member participa-tion in trade union affairs in Britain. The interests of the great bulk of Jugoslavian industrial workers, that is to say, are deter-mined by the fact that they form a class of life-long manual workers, permanently subject to the day-to-day commands of the director of the enterprise and his representatives in super-vision, with interests different from theirs. For this reason it is open to question whether the classical form of capitalism has been replaced by a new type of class society, the collectivist, since the directors, along with the full-time politicians and administrators, also form a class who will direct, rather than do, manual work for the whole of their occupied lives. Rank-and-file participation, whether through Workers' Councils as in the Jugoslavian case, or through trade union branches, works' com-mittees and Communist Party branches as in the Russian, may be seen from this point of view as a kind of parallel to joint industrial councils, joint consultation committees and human relations policies through personnel departments in the British. They are, that is, means by which to obtain the integrated labour force necessary for modern large-scale production (Banks, 1970). The divergent roles played by workers and managers in production produce 'the inevitable stream of complaints' which the Webbs saw in the Russian system but failed to interpret because they did not appreciate that collective ownership does not preclude class conflict, albeit a different kind of class con-flict from that which prevails under private enterprise.

Thus in purely formal terms the system of role relationships, derived from Dunlop's analysis and summed up schematically above (p. 21) can be seen to be operative in both the British and the Communist case, but the content of the role obligations is very different, because of the different ideologies which operate. The introduction of Workers' Councils for example, complicates the clarity of trade union participation in the system, since some negotiating functions are carried out by the Workers' Council representative and it is not clear whether there are clearly worked out spheres of interest which separate his from those of the trade-union representative. Negotiations take place also with regard to different issues. Wages and hours of work, to be sure, are common to all systems; but the responsibility of the enterprise for housing, for example, gives the Communist nego-tiators a set of responsibilities not shared by their British counterparts. Nevertheless, the striking feature of all systems is the extent to which the shop-floor representative has emerged as a vital role in modern times. In part this may have been the result of the growing need in large-scale enterprise for managers to have a more direct contact with the shop than their office routines normally permit. In part, however, it may have come from the activities of trade unions themselves, seeking to change the economic system towards one more responsive to the require-ments of the individual workers. A more complete understand-ing of the emergence of the role of shop steward in British industry and of the shop-floor representative in the Communist societies depends upon a more detailed consideration of trade unionism as a social movement. The next part of this book accordingly deals with trade unions as instruments of social change.

PART 2:

Instrument of
Social Change

CHAPTER V

The Sociology of the
Trade Union Movement

The sociologist who sets out to examine the degree to which
trade unions are instruments of social change must avoid two
extreme theoretical dogmas which have bedevilled the literature
on this topic. Some authors, bemused by the obvious fact that
so many changes in social life occur which are not only unintended but positively disliked by the people who experience
them, write as though they believe all social changes to be of
this type. The ebb and flow of participation in, and of activities
by, the trade union movement are seen, from this point of view,
as no more than a response to 'underlying' economic, political
and other social events which take place independently of trade
unionists' efforts. Thus, Tannenbaum has asserted that 'the
original organizer of the trade union movement is the shop,
the factory, the mine, and the industry. The agitator or the
labour leader merely announces the already existing fact.' The
industrial revolution destroyed the traditional community in
work which the medieval guild provided. Hence the trade union
emerged as the 'spontaneous grouping of individual workers
thrown together functionally. It reflects the moral identity and
psychological unity men always discover when they work together.' In brief, 'the organization of workers is essential in a
modern industrial society, and if unionism did not exist it would
have to be invented' (Tannenbaum, 1952).

Similarly, Smelser's interpretation turns on the notion that
the industrial revolution and the separation of home from work
resulted in a new family structure. 'As part of this process,
several of the family's functions began to slip away. To take
over these old functions, complementary organizations began
to appear.' Once the members of families regularly offered their

labour services to employers outside the family and away from its location, a body became necessary to mediate between the family 'and its industrial pursuits'. This body was the trade union (Smelser, 1959).

From the functionalist, as from the economic organizational point of view, that is to say, a trade union movement is no more than a creature of social changes which have been produced by other means, for all that its members and partisans may desire and intend to create a new world order themselves. A trade union comes into existence to fill a void caused by innovations which represent a break with the past, but it has no power to innovate of its own volition. What it does achieve, and all that it can achieve, is to satisfy the requirements of the new system. The desires, intentions, aims, objects, purposes of trade unionists are of no avail beyond this. They no doubt reflect stresses and strains and dissatisfactions with the way industry is organized and the place of the worker in society, and in this sense they may be read as symptoms of the deeper disturbances which are occurring in the industrial system; but the working out of these disturbances and the establishment of new forms of economic relationships are not within the capacity of trade unions to achieve. The sociologist must look elsewhere for an understanding of these processes and an explanation of what decides their course.

In contrast to this deterministic conception of social change some authors have expressed a wholly voluntaristic one. From this point of view the salient fact in the present context is that 'the period in which Unions have grown has witnessed a great improvement in the whole economic condition of the classes which have formed them'. Union militancy is seen as essentially a causal factor in this process, trade union action or perhaps the action of a more general labour movement of which the trade unions are part, being held responsible for the improvement. From an examination of trade union successes, 'instances in which the Unions have actually agitated or fought with success', such an argument moves on to explain away failures—'though the Union may be defeated the fight may be justified by results'. Open conflict in any case is held to be of marginal significance. 'The best-drilled, most effective union does not fight because it has no need. It is by the steady pressure of organized opinion, by the delicate tact of skilled negotiations, by the quietly effective ways about which newspapers are silent, that the best work is done' (Hobhouse, 1906). Hence an understanding of the course of trade union history depends on establishing beyond dispute what the actual aims and methods of trade unionists are. What they are working for is fundamental to what they achieve.

A negative form of the voluntaristic conception of trade union activity has also been expressed by radicals, like Marx and Lenin, in their attempts to get workers' organizations to espouse the cause of revolutionary communism (Banks, 1970). The workers of the world would unite, it has been believed, if only their trade unions could be so moved to reveal the true nature of the capitalist opposition. 'Marx and Lenin, when defining the trade unions, did not think that *all* trade unions, at all times and in all countries, were schools of communism. They spoke only about those unions *which carry on the class struggle against the capitalists and the capitalist system.*' (Lozovsky, 1935.) Without class consciousness and the will to revolution, it has been argued more recently, trade union leaders 'simply act as transmission belts of capitalism within the proletariat'. Such leaders are 'mediocre, authoritarian and conformist, and their members have in consequence a low level of political consciousness' (Anderson, 1967). Presumably, militancy on the part of trade unions not only means that they will become engaged in *political* rather than merely industrial struggles, but that these struggles *will be successful*. Of course, in their more cautious moments such authors admit that there are limitations to what a trade union movement can achieve, just as the determinists admit to the possibility that some freedom of action occurs, but since neither party examines the significance of these admissions the reader is left with the impression that explanation of trade union behaviour is held to be best expressed in terms of the extreme. The history of the trade union movement is either a response to changes which occur and which are beyond the power of trade unionists to achieve or a record of the way in which everything achieved was a consequence of all that was wanted.

Since the evidence presented by authors taking one or other of the extreme points of view is impressive, neither can be true. The task of the sociologist, accordingly, is to think of social movements in a manner which will allow for the recurrence of unanticipated, unintended and unwanted processes of social change alongside deliberate and successful attempts to bring about desired modifications of practice. The problem, in brief, is to devise a theory which will indicate just how much of history is determined by processes beyond human control and how much is consciously willed; and one approach to this problem consists in a step-by-step analysis of the trial and error progression which men use in their efforts to create something new from whatever features of their circumstances they find amenable to manipulation. From this point of view, a trade union movement is a *socially constructive* grouping of organizations whose activities may be defined in terms of objectives, shared by their members, provided it is understood that sometimes these objectives are achieved, but also that others are given up when they are seen as no longer relevant or no longer desirable in the new circumstances which have arisen. This conception puts the diffusion of a social innovation on the same theoretical level as the diffusion of any other kind of innovation for which men have been responsible in their experiments to convert an idea of what might possibly be into an actuality (Banks, 1972).

For example, the elaborate constitution of the Amalgamated Society of Engineers seems to have been largely the work of the two trade union leaders, William Allan and William Newton. Among other things they framed a detailed financial and administrative system 'which enabled the Union to combine the functions of a trade protection society with those of a permanent insurance company, and thus attain a financial stability hitherto undreamt of'. But they were not content with invention merely. 'Newton and Allan appear, indeed, to have eagerly seized every opportunity for writing letters to the newspapers, reading papers, and delivering lectures about the organization which they had established.' (S. and B. Webb, 1894.) This advocacy on their part parallels the publicity which accompanies the exploitation of an invention in the mechanical arts, and it resulted in the constitution of the Amalgamated becoming adopted, in whole or in part, by many other British trade unions between 1852 and 1875. There thus appeared in the history of trade unionism in this country the 'New Model', an exclusive organization of the aristocracy of the skilled workmen, which accumulated members and money and forced employers to recognize the trade union as a perpetual opposition with which they must bargain rather than as an alternative government which they must never permit to exist. As opposed to the 'universal' principle of organization which sought in the 1830's to establish a general union of men of all trades (Cole, 1953), the 'New Model' constituted a device to cope with the employers' definition of the industrial world as composed of occupations of varying degrees of skill for which different wages must be paid, while achieving co-ordination for political action through the organization locally of the Trades Councils. The failure of general unionism may thus be said to be symptomatic of the fact that desire alone will not result in a revolutionary new order, 'a new heaven and a new earth' (S. and B. Webb, 1894). The success of the 'New Model' indicates how innovation in the social, as in the material world, takes its point of departure from the nature of the circumstances with which men have to cope.

In an earlier chapter, on the sociology of industrial relations systems, four sets of 'givens' were identified as stamping a particular impression on the relationship between the role-players in these systems and dominating the kinds of rules which they establish to guide their conduct in the workplace. These are:

(1) the technical and social characteristics of the workplace,
(2) the market constraints on the enterprise,
(3) the power of the actors in the wider society, and
(4) the system of property ownership which decides who is to direct operations.

Although from the angle of collective bargaining each of these variables is a 'stubborn' fact, conditioning the kinds of bargains to be made, from the angle of trade unionism as an instrument of social change it is a focus of challenge and inventiveness. Productivity bargaining is perhaps a case in point with respect to the first of these in Britain today. Defined as 'an agreement in which advantages of one kind or another, such as higher wages or increased leisure, are given to workers in return for agreement on their part to accept changes in working practice or in methods or in organization of work which will lead to more efficient working', productivity bargaining has been much in evidence in recent times as a device by which employers may meet the rising labour costs attendant on full employment. The initiative for such bargaining, that is to say, has usually come from the employers. Nevertheless, some British trade unions, notably the Transport and General Workers' Union, have been said to pursue the policy of persuading laggardly employers to enter into negotiations of this nature (Donovan Secretariat, 1967), and, to the degree that they have been successful, they may be claimed consciously and deliberately to have altered some aspects of the technical and social characteristics of the workplace. In particular, the specification of working practices in written agreements 'for whose enforcement and observations the unions accepted a joint responsibility with the company' (Flanders, 1964) represents an innovation in British workplace practice which trade union leaders have often wanted, even if they had not worked for them themselves, and which they have been ready to accept on the employers' initiative.

Yet, although the history of the trade union movement reveals some examples of innovation in workplace practice, brought about directly by the pressure of unions on employers, by far the greatest impact has been made elsewhere, on the government as an agency which *intervenes* between managers and workers in their industrial relations systems. An obvious case in point is the nationalization of the British coal industry. Raised initially at the Trades Union Congress of 1892 by representatives of the Lanarkshire miners, it became official policy of the Miners' Federation in 1894; and the Labour Group which entered Parliament in 1906 adopted the nationalization of the mines as part of its programme. Thereafter it remained part of the policy programmes of the T.U.C. and the Labour Party until it became law. A Miners' Federation Bill for nationalizing mines and minerals was defeated in the House of Commons by 264 votes to 168 but this was a Private Members' Bill, sponsored by the minority Labour Government of the day, and not a government measure. Another attempt was made, this time by the Labour Party in opposition, in 1937 and this was also defeated, by 182 votes to 125. At the end of the Second World War the miners, the T.U.C. and the Labour Party were united in their determination to nationalize the coal industry and this was achieved in 1946 (Barry, 1965). This is a clear example of how the trade union movement campaigned not merely for a change in the system of property ownership but also for changes in the market situation of the industry as well as in the social characteristics of each workplace. The Act of Nationalization created a single enterprise, a monopoly by contrast to the 750 separate, competing undertakings which existed in 1946. At every level of the industry, right up to the top, representatives of the National Union of Miners were empowered to sit on joint committees with representatives of the management to solve problems which had previously been regarded as management prerogative in the industry.

In brief, for over seventy years, miners' leaders had struggled unsuccessfully to persuade mine owners to form with them a national machine for the settlement of disputes to replace the district boards which the owners preferred. Now, by the simple Act of Nationalization, this was achieved. Of course, there were many years of preparation by the miners to get the Act passed. They had first to persuade the Trades Union Congress that public ownership of the coal mines was both desirable and workable. They then had to persuade the Labour Party to accept such a measure as part of its programme, and to convince politicians in other Parties of the wisdom of the course. The mining trade unions and the T.U.C., along with them, acted throughout as a *cause* pressure group movement, one which operates on the principle that governments *should* modify some existing operations or establish entirely fresh agencies to realize the aims espoused by the movement (Banks, 1972). They did not expect to take over these constructive tasks themselves, however much they were anxious to participate in them as partners with whatever types of managers the government might establish. The Act of Nationalization in this sense confirmed the expectations of the movement. It did not put an end to the trade unions in the industry as it did to private ownership; instead, it set up a National Coal Board and subsidiary bodies, with defined functions, in partnership with trade unions who are intended to continue to be the 'permanent opposition' they had been before nationalization (Clegg, 1951).

This description of the trade union movement as a 'cause' pressure group movement serves to draw attention to the dis-

tinction between its aims at various times, its methods of procedure, its tactics and strategies, and those of other pressure
groups on the one hand, and its difference from other types of
social movement on the other. Not all pressure groups, that is to
say, have causes to pursue. Some groups seek to influence public
policy only intermittently, whenever they have a social or an
economic interest which they think is threatened or may be
enhanced by some proposed state measure. The Federation
of British Industries was a pressure group in this sense, as is the
T.U.C., to the degree that many of the issues which it raises
with government departments and with Members of Parliament
are solely concerned with the immediate present. But to the
degree that the T.U.C. has beliefs or principles which impel
it to pressure the government to pass legislation, to make
administrative orders, or in other ways to impose a *new social
order* from above, it is a 'cause' pressure group. Not all social
movements, however, work in this way. 'Self-help' social movements, of which the Co-operative Movement is the clearest
example, seek to create the new social order directly within
existing societies, by demonstrating practically how people
themselves may organize the new way of running affairs for
themselves. Trade unions have, to be sure, occasionally espoused
the self-help form. During the 1830's, for example, some British
trade unions opened workshops where members who were unemployed or on strike could be occupied co-operatively to produce goods for their maintenance (Cole, 1953). This Owenite
phase was, however, short-lived and the expansion of the Co-
operative Movement in this country has been accompanied by
the growth of trade unions for shop and other workers, and for
Co-operative managers and officials (Cole, 1944), which regard
the Movement in much the same fashion as their counterparts
for private and state enterprises regard the employers in those
spheres.

Trade unions have also from time to time supported revolutionary ideas and have put on the mantle of the revolutionary
social movement, seeking to take over the state, by force if
necessary, or by a general strike of all workers, in order to
destroy the existing social system and to establish a new one
from above; the leaders of the movement themselves have
formed the government for the innovating regime (Banks, 1972).

But trade unions have rarely espoused this policy for long or with much enthusiasm, even in societies where such revolutions have occurred. Thus, the Russian trade unions played an 'auxiliary role' in the general strike and unsuccessful attempt at rebellion in 1905 and a even more minor role in the October revolution of 1917 (Deutscher, 1950). Neither the self-help nor the revolutionary social movement form accords with the self-image of the trade unionist as promoter of social change. Just as collective bargaining implies the continued existence of a separate employer with whom the trade union will bargain, so the pressure group conception of the instrument by which causes are pursued implies the continued existence of a separate government on which the trade union will exert pressure. Clearly, individual trade unionists and trade union leaders may envisage a society without employers or governments, but such a society must also be one without trade unions in the sense in which such organizations operate in the industrial world of today.

The Russian example is illuminating in this context. When the Bolsheviks abandoned the 'mixed economy' and embarked upon rapid industrialization from the centre and the collectivization of farming with Stalin's first five year plan in 1928, the eighth Congress of Trade Unions reported that frictions between the trade unions and the economic administration had increased and that unofficial strikes were troubling industry. Some of the trade union leaders saw this unrest as evidence that the unions had been failing in their responsibilities to their members and asserted that their first duty was to press for increased wages and better conditions. The government, on the other hand, stood by its conviction that the productivity of labour must rise more quickly than wages if there were to be a significantly large surplus to permit increasing industrialization and called upon the trade unions to promote 'socialist competition' amongst workers and to organize 'shock brigades' to this end (S. and B. Webb, 1935). In order to cope with the union leaders' challenge, indeed, the Bolsheviks held a closed session of their delegates to the Congress which resulted in their ensuring that only men who supported the industrialization drive were elected to the Central Council of Trade Unions. A subsequent 'purge' of the unions made certain that the Five Year Plans would have their wholehearted support (Deutscher, 1950).

This should not be interpreted to mean that the trade unions in Russia ceased thereafter to have any influence on the government. Rather should this action be understood as a re-definition of their sphere of influence. As was mentioned in the last chapter, wage rates and co-efficients, which differentiate between jobs in terms of the quality of the work done, are decided centrally by a government agency which discusses proposals to make changes with the All-Union Central Council of Trade Unions; and although it is not known publicly how much influence, or how little, is exerted by the union leaders at this level, the opportunity is clearly there for them to express points of view about the wisdom of proposals and to put forward proposals of their own, in much the same manner as trade union leaders in Britain discuss policy with government departments. Similarly, their responsibility for welfare and housing in the Russian system makes it possible for them to influence the government directly on behalf of their members, simply because they have been charged with this duty, whereas in Britain these issues are dealt with by government and quasi-government agencies subject to pressure through parliament. A pressure group, that is to say, can exert as much pressure as a government is prepared to tolerate and no more, and it can exert this pressure only along those lines which the government defines as legitimate. Hence, the skill of the leaders of such a group can be judged by the degree to which they can succeed in getting their opinions accepted even in situations apparently unfavourable to their reception and in shifts of circumstance which are apparently to their disadvantage. One of the main tasks of a sociology of these movements is to show how the unanticipated, unintended and unwanted processes of social change result in variations of endeavour on the part of the leaders and members of the organized movement, seeking always to achieve its major goals, the 'cause' for which it stands.

The identification of such a cause is both essential, therefore, and difficult, largely because it has to be inferred from the actions taken by trade unionists in their unwillingness merely to respond to the challenges of the moment. The constructive element implies that members and partisans have long-term objectives in mind. Yet the expressed goals are rarely illuminating. As the Webbs pointed out, the printed rule books of English trade unions contain a 'comprehensive' truism—'the chief object of our society is to elevate the social position of our members'— which is so comprehensive and general that it is not very enlightening. 'Drafted originally by enthusiastic pioneers, copied and recopied by successive revising committees, the printed constitutions of working class associations represent rather the aspirations than the everyday action of the members' (S. and B. Webb, 1898). The sociologist must perforce attempt to infer the aspirations from enduring actions. For example, the trade union struggle to remove legal constraints on *collective* bargaining implies, in all industrial societies, a rejection of the classical capitalist conception of economic organization. In place of unfettered, individual competition the trade unions worked for, and apparently desire to continue, a system of collective regulation in the detailed, day-to-day application of which their representatives will play an important role. At the same time, the fact that this is conceived as collective *bargaining* means that the sale and purchase of labour power will continue into the foreseeable future. The wages system is to be perpetuated, so that even where the capitalist is abolished, as in a nationalized industry or in a completely nationalized economy, bargaining over wages will continue to be a major union function. Trade unions, it may be said, prefer a collective to an individual employer, but they always assume there will be an employer to bargain with. There is no question of their members sharing the employer's role amongst themselves. The elevation of the social position of the rank and file does not mean this. Rather does it mean a steady rise in the level of living of the worker. Hence, in the British context, the demand for a minimum wage level, never to be eroded by rising costs of living, has been accompanied by trade union agitation for improved benefits and services by a welfare state, to which employers are entitled as much as workers. Beyond the minimum, however, there is no demand for equality. The trade union toleration of differentials in wage bargains, in Russia as in Britain, and an emphasis on merit as a reason for them (Wootton, 1955) indicates at best an aspiration for a wages structure which gives equal remuneration for work of equal value. 'To each according to his deeds' is a more accurate rendering of the trade union slogan than 'to each according to his needs'; so that while there is a drive to satisfy minimum needs for all, employers are considered to make more of a contribution to the collective product than their workers.

Within the confines of such an analysis as this, then, the sociologist seeks to understand how it is that trade union leaders, trade union members and trade union supporters go about the business of putting pressure on employers and governments. In particular he is careful to examine their reactions to unforeseen circumstances, their search for allies at home and abroad in their enduring attempts to raise the social level of the worker in industrial societies. In a book of this length, of course, it is not possible to carry out such an analysis in detail, and, as in the previous section, a striking feature of the contemporary British scene has been chosen for more detailed examination. Just as the trade union as an instrument of collective bargaining was approached through a consideration of the emerging role of the shop steward as the link between managers and workers, so the trade union as an instrument of social change will be examined by reference to the trade union leader as a member of the 'establishment', a link man between government departments and the associations of the working class.

CHAPTER VI

Welfare Unionism in Britain

In its Evidence to the Royal Commission on Trade Unions and Employers' Associations the Trade Union Congress stated the objectives of trade unionism to be:

(1) improved terms of employment
(2) improved physical environment at work
(3) full employment and national prosperity
(4) security of employment and income
(5) improved social security
(6) fair shares in national income and wealth
(7) industrial democracy
(8) a voice in government
(9) improved public and social services
(10) public control and planning of industry
    (Trades Union Congress, 1966)

Most of these objectives are clearly beyond the reach of collective bargaining between employers and trade unions in the English industrial relations system. They indicate therefore the degree to which the T.U.C. leaders conceive of the trade union movement in Britain as a pressure group 'cause' movement in the sense of the previous chapter. Indeed, the second objective in the list must also be thought of in these terms because in the *Evidence* the T.U.C. asserted that many of the improvements in safety and health and other aspects of physical working conditions 'can best be brought about by the Government laying down minimum standards. If they are not achieved through collective bargaining, this does not therefore indicate that these matters are low on the list of trade union priorities.

63

If they can best be dealt with by statutory regulation, trade unions will pursue the method of pressure on Government to achieve their objectives in this field.' What collective bargaining can achieve, even in industry itself, seems to be seen by the T.U.C. as remarkably limited. To achieve its objectives a trade union movement must undertake political action.

There is nothing novel about this conception of trade unionism. The T.U.C. in 1966 was in fact following in this respect the line its predecessors had followed for the past 100 years. When the first Congress met, in 1868, it passed a resolution which declared it to be 'highly desirable that the trades of the United Kingdom should hold an annual congress for the purpose of bringing the trades into a closer alliance, and to take action in all parliamentary matters pertaining to the general interests of the working classes'. The first Trades Union Congresses were in consequence almost wholly concerned with the relevant political issues of the day—the Report of the Royal Commission on Trade Unions of 1869 and the subsequent Trade Union Act of 1871—and it is significant that the first standing Committee of the new organization was called the 'Parliamentary Committee', set up initially in 1871 'to watch over the passage of the Trade Union Bill'. By half a century later the Parliamentary Committee of the T.U.C. had become 'a powerful pressure group recognized by all parties and treated by all Governments as the authoritative spokesman of the opinions of organized labour' (Roberts, 1958); and the General Council of the T.U.C., which replaced it in 1921, continued to perform this task.

For the most part the members of the General Council are the chief executive officers of the member unions of the T.U.C. For example, only two of the 36 members of the General Council in 1965-66 were not full-time officers of their unions (Trades Union Congress, 1966). This means that the focus of pressure group activity on the part of the Trade Union Movement is organized by a very restricted section of the total union body, men who spend the whole of their working day in administration and sitting on committees with other trade unionists, with representatives of employers, with civil servants and with other representatives of government agencies. Indeed, the growing importance of contact between the T.U.C. and this last group is made manifest by the facts that, whereas in 1931-32 the T.U.C.

was represented on only one government committee, by 1938-39 this number had risen to 12, by 1948-49 to 60 and by 1957-58 to 65 (Allen, 1960). Over this same period the number of Trade Union-sponsored Members of Parliament fluctuated from 35 (General election of 1931) to 78 (1935) to 111 (1950) to 92 (1959). These figures, obviously, do not allow for the changing fortunes of the Labour Party in these elections. Altogether 46 Labour M.P's were retained in 1931, 154 in 1935, 315 in 1950 and 258 in 1959 (Butler and Freeman, 1969) so that the *proportion* of trade union M.P's in the Parliamentary Labour Party fell from 76.1% in 1931 to 50.6% (1935) to 35.2% (1950) and rose slightly to 35.7% in 1959. A growth in membership of government committees on the part of trade union leaders has, it appears, been accompanied by a decline in representation in the House of Commons. The import of this for the operation of trade unions as a pressure group movement needs further clarification.

When the Labour Representation Committee was established in 1900 only 41 trade unions out of 1,272 joined with the Fabian Society, the Social Democratic Federation, the Socialist League and the Independent Labour Party to form what a journalist of the day called 'a little cloud, no bigger than a man's hand, which may grow into a United Labour Party'. It is true that it was the larger trade unions which were involved but even so their total affiliated membership amounted to only 353,070 out of an aggregate trade union membership in Britain of 1,905,116 (Pelling, 1965). However, by the General Election of 1906 the number of trade unions affiliated to the L.R.C. had risen to 158, representing 904,496 trade union members. For this election the Parliamentary Committee of the T.U.C. issued a statement, asking all trade unionists and wage earners to vote only for candidates who were pledged to support a whole series of measures, mostly of direct interest to trade union activists but also including the more general welfare proposals of the establishment of a State Pension Fund at 60 years of age and an extension of the Housing of the Working Classes Act, as well as the 'feminist' political demand for adult suffrage. In the event some 30 L.R.C. members were returned to the House of Commons by the election. 23 of these were trade unionists. In addition 17 other Members of this Parliament were trade union members, sponsored independently, 13 of them miners (Clegg *et al.*, 1964). Thus, when the L.R.C. became the Labour Party, later in the year, its trade union 'contingent' was a major part of its force in parliamentary politics; and this pattern was repeated at every General Election until that of 1945.

At the 1945 election, to be sure, as many as 120 of the 124 trade union-sponsored candidates were successful at the polls but the total number of Labour M.P's was 393, many of them returned by constituencies in which the working-class electorate was relatively small. 'The change was unmistakeable. Into the House came a flood of middle class Members, often straight from the services, with little experience of the trade union movement. Throughout the 1945 Parliament the influence of the trade union M.P's steadily declined, although they still included most of the veterans.' (Harrison, 1960.) Of course, at this time the influence of those veterans in the Labour Parliament was still important—six of Mr. Attlee's twenty-member strong first Cabinet were union-sponsored M.P's and he selected a further 23 from amongst their ranks to fill government posts without a seat in the Cabinet. By 1951, however, these figures had dwindled to 4 and 18 respectively. 'This decline was due to a shortage of competent trade unionists upon whom Mr. Attlee could call to fill vacancies. Mr. Attlee had his preferences (for Old Haileyburians, sc) but he would not have disregarded trade unionists of marked political ability in favour of lesser men with public school and university backgrounds.' (Allen, 1960.) Nevertheless, by 1951 the most prominent members of the Labour government were younger men, without a trade union background, who were university educated. Subsequent Labour governments appear to have maintained this preference.

In his analysis of the causes for this decline in trade union representation in the legislative and executive organs of British government Harrison points to the extent to which the Labour Party since the Second World War has ceased to be 'a *labour* party'. Although very many Labour M.P's are still recruited from amongst the ranks of those who are born to and reared in working class families, more and more their occupations *at the time of entering* the House of Commons have been professional or non-manual generally. The trade union-sponsored candidate is no longer so attractive to the constituency party. Nevertheless, much more prominent in his analysis than this emphasis on change within the Party itself is the indication that the trade unions for the most part are not so eager to remain a Parliamentary force that they are prepared to take the necessary steps to ensure their representation. Of course, some trade unionists have expressed irritation at losing nominations and have complained to the National Executive Committee of the Labour Party and, at the Party's Annual Conference, have complained about the change of mood in the constituency organizations, but on the whole the unions seem ambivalent about the worth of Parliamentary representation at the present time (Harrison, 1960). They have not switched their allegiance from the Labour Party to some other political party but have grown accustomed to exercising their pressure elsewhere in the administrative system.

This new outlook on the part of union leaders is perhaps best exemplified by the fact that almost immediately after the General Election in October 1951, when the Conservatives were returned to power, the T.U.C. issued a statement which asserted that it would 'seek to work amicably with whatever Government is in power and, through consultation jointly with Ministers ... to find practical solutions to the social and economic problems facing this country. There need be no doubt, therefore, of the attitude of the T.U.C. towards the new Government. In joint consultation and in all other activities it will be our constant aim and duty to ensure the steady progress and betterment of the general condition of Britain and of our people. We shall continue in that duty under a Conservative Government.' (Quoted in Roberts, 1961.) Critics of the T.U.C. General Council saw this as a departure from principle. 'It revealed that in the minds of the T.U.C. leaders a victorious Tory Government was as good as a defeated Labour Government any day.' (Roberts, 1961.) But even a brief examination of the record of the five years of Labour government between 1945 and 1950 reveals that by the time of the 1951 General Election so many links had been established between the T.U.C. and government departments that there was every expectation *on all sides* that in the vast administrative machine of the Welfare State trade union representation, and the opinion of trade union leaders, had an important role to play which would not be served by their withdrawal from all co-operation with the government.

By this time, that is to say, trade union objectives could be seen to be helped forward more by union leaders going directly to the relevant government official rather than by making use of their union M.P's. At this time, for example, the Transport and General Workers' Union 'tended to use the Members of Parliament on its panel less for dealing with Union political problems and more for handling the problems of individual members of the Union' (Allen, 1957). Twenty years later the General Council of the T.U.C. followed another Conservative victory in June, 1970 with the statement that 'over the years, consultation between the Government and both sides of industry has been extended in range and depth and the T.U.C. expects of the new Government that they will maintain this development. . . . Advice about the way to tackle the social, economic and industrial problems of this country will be readily available to this Government, as it was to previous Governments' (Trade Union Congress, 1970). If, indeed, the total number of trade union representatives on administrative and other government committees has been less under Conservative as compared with Labour administrations, the reason is because the former tend to rely less on such committees and not because they have reduced the T.U.C. share of representation (Allen, 1960).

Altogether, then, the trade union leaders have come to regard their personal participation in government committee work as a more effective means of securing the trade union movement's welfare and industrial aims than delegated participation in the legislative process through trade union M.P's. This change of emphasis on their part should not be regarded as a simple case of either sycophantic apostasy or blatant error. The nature of modern British government is such that many more decisions are made administratively than politically, and, as Thoenes has put it, 'the fact that in the Welfare State a great number of decisions of an administrative character by-pass the government machine does not mean that they are low-level decisions. Issues which were once the topic of heated and prolonged political debate have nowadays come to be regarded, however incorrectly, as technical problems for which the relevant expertise is not oratory but executive finesse.' (Thoenes, 1966.) Top civil servants and trade union officials alike appreciate such finesse in each other's ranks. Since a 'cause' pressure group movement always seeks to put its endeavours where they appear to be likely to have most effect, the second half of twentieth-century Britain has witnessed the leaders of such movements, trade unionists amongst them, walking the corridors of Whitehall rather than those of Westminster; and the more influential of them are those who sit regularly on those committees whose decisions have far-reaching consequences.

Of course, this new sphere of activity has brought its own problems for the movement. Trade union leaders are busy men. The management of the affairs of their own unions, attendance at executive and other committee meetings, conferences, nego-tiations, dealing with official and unofficial strikes, with adminis-trative problems, and the constant demand to address meetings up and down the country take up much of their time. In addi-tion, the top leaders of the movement have to attend the meet-ings of the General Council of the T.U.C. and its committees, as well as meetings of the Federations and similar bodies to which they belong. Some of them sit on Government advisory bodies and the other 100 or so outside committees on which the T.U.C. is represented, and from time to time they are appointed to Courts of Inquiry or to Royal Commissions or as part-time mem-bers of Boards of the nationalized industries. On behalf of the T.U.C. some of them will also be required to attend international trade union meetings and other conferences abroad—'every summer the business of the General Council languishes while ten or so of its members spend five weeks at the International Labour Conference' (Wigham, 1961). Small wonder, then, that this pres-sure of work results in the T.U.C. representatives sometimes acting 'in a limited and somewhat negative fashion' on govern-ment committees 'preventing decisions being taken which are inimical to the interests of trade unions more by being present than by argument' (Allen, 1960); and it is clearly open to ques-tion how far this fragmentation of the trade union leader's activities prevents him from being as effective an innovator for the movement as he might be with rather more time at his dis-posal for exerting pressure, or indeed, as his predecessors perhaps were when they shared lobbying with the trade union M.P's and members of the Parliamentary Labour Party generally.

In terms of the analysis presented in the previous chapter, that is to say, the development of Welfare administration since the Second World War has produced unanticipated and unintended consequences for the organization of the trade union movement in Britain which make it difficult for the T.U.C. leaders to demonstrate publicly whether or not they are effective social innovators; and the general feature of administration by and through government departments, that it is 'as far as the general public is concerned—faceless, voiceless, unidentifiable, in brief, anonymous' (Finer, 1958), can easily be misinterpreted to mean in this context that the trade union leaders are not in fact successfully pursuing, or have lost all desire to pursue, the movement's long-term objectives. The campaigns for the nationalization of certain industries apart, however, it is doubtful whether the trade union movement was any more effective when it worked mainly through the Labour Party and the House of Commons in the full glare of newspaper publicity than it is now in the quiet offices and committee rooms of the Ministries, and as the case of nationalization itself demonstrates, the mere passing of legislation is no more than the first step in transforming the organization of an industry. To make the nationalized industries work to the advantage of the public generally and to the advantage of their members in particular trade union leaders must perforce spend much of their time on the Boards and other committees responsible for administering these industries on behalf of the government. The price of effective pressure group practice, it seems, is eternal attention to detail on the part of the leaders of a movement.

The ambivalence of the trade unions to the traditional policy of maintaining a panel of parliamentary candidates to fight elections as members of the Labour Party is demonstrated, moreover, not only in the attitude of their leaders to participation in the committees of administration of the Welfare State when the Conservative Party is in power but also in the attitude of the rank-and-file members to political involvement by their union. Although the evidence of a sample survey, conducted in 1962 to 1964, showed that trade union members' votes went seven to three in favour of the Labour Party in the 1964 election, only a third of the trade unionists thought that trade unions should have close ties with the Labour Party and 65% said that trade unions should stay out of politics. No doubt, as the researchers themselves claimed, part of the explanation for the desire to dissociate the unions from the Party arose from memories of the Labour Government's confrontations with the unions over a wages policy sixteen years earlier (Butler and Stokes, 1969, Chapter 7), and similarly, part of the support for the Labour Party in the election came from disillusionment with 13 years of Conservative rule. Yet it is also likely that, as another study has put it, the average rank-and-file trade unionist sees his interests as primarily bound up in earnings and what they will purchase. By such members 'the trade union is seen almost exclusively as a means of improving their standard of living, and not as an agency for transforming the social structure' (Goldthorpe, *et al.*, 1968). Their conception of membership of a trade union, that is to say, does not carry the connotation of partisanship to a cause beyond the realms of the collective bargaining process. To the degree that they favour some measures of social change, their voting for the Labour Party may well be interpreted as a choice of the most likely agency for such purposes, but voting for Labour candidates and paying trade union subscriptions are seen as two quite distinct operations that have nothing to do with each other. Only the minority of militants who think of themselves as involved in a world-wide, or at least a nation-wide, struggle to achieve a more desirable economic and social system look upon the two activities as intimately related, although even the militants may well doubt whether parliamentary action through the Labour Party is the most appropriate means for this purpose at the present time. Within a single trade union, in other words, there will be varying degrees of commitment to the general principles and ideology of trade unionism at different times.

This draws attention back to the criteria of such commitment as set out in Chapter I. Clearly, British trade unions not only vary within themselves but between themselves in the extent to which they subscribe to all or few of the indices of unionateness, listed by Blackburn and Prandy (Blackburn and Prandy, 1965, Blackburn, 1967). Some unions prefer not to court possible unpopularity and eschew the word 'union' altogether from their titles, calling themselves 'guilds' or 'associations'. Others who are not so worried by the form of words nevertheless do not register as trade unions. Yet others do not affiliate to the Trades Union Congress. For example, of the 280 'purely' white-collar trade unions identified in 1964 only 43 were affiliated to the T.U.C., although admittedly these were the major ones. Not all of these were further affiliated to the Labour Party, but this was also true of manual workers' unions (Bain, 1970). Insofar as the concept of the trade union *movement* in Britain entails *collective* action through the T.U.C. *and* the Labour Party to achieve objectives like those set out in the *Evidence* of the T.U.C. to the Royal Commission, some trade unions and trade unionists may be said not to be part of such a movement at all. Nor is it immediately obvious that these trade union members see themselves as part of some other movement with different objectives, although in their capacities other than as trade unionists they may be members of a political party, a religious body with explicit social goals to achieve, or another organization with a cause to pursue. Trade unionism for these people is 'business' unionism, concerned like that of any other business philosophy with the single-minded pursuit of gain. The problem indeed, for the trade union leader who thinks of his role in the wider terms is how to reconcile his welfare activities on behalf of the T.U.C., the Trade Union Movement, the Working Class, and humanity eventually, with dogged persistence on behalf of the sectional interests of his own union's members, especially when they appear to be incompatible with the general good. A sociology of social movements, which emphasizes the trial and error nature of the progression of trade unionism, must also emphasize the degree to which trade union leaders are successful in their attempts at such reconciliation. It must also, however, consider the degree to which 'pure' business unionism is also forced to compromise with the welfare tendencies of modern industrial society. An example of this will be considered in the next chapter.

CHAPTER VII

Business Unionism in America

The I.L.O. Mission to study the trade union situation in the United States of America in 1959 reported that it 'was struck in its discussions with union leaders by the almost total absence of any questioning of the bases of the American economic and social system. Unlike many labour movements in Europe and elsewhere, the trade unions in the United States do not appear even to consider, still less to advocate, any major change in the system in which they operate, in spite of the many bitter battles that have occurred between unions and capital' (International Labour office, 1960a). In particular, the failure of the American trade unions to participate in the founding and running of a reformist labour party and their insistence on working for limited objectives and immediate improvements in the conditions of work and wages of their members suggest that they lack an essential element of unionateness, in Blackburn's sense of that term (Blackburn, 1967). Yet, as the Mission itself emphasized, trade union leaders sit regularly on advisory committees set up by almost every agency of the federal government, and they have lobbied Congress and the State legislatures on issues of trade union concern for a very long time. The striking feature of business unionism in America, that is to say, is not that it eschews political action altogether but that it gives every impression of undertaking pressure group activity which is interest oriented rather than directed towards the pursuit of causes (Bell, 1958).

The lack of trade union enthusiasm for a 'third' political party should not be misunderstood. Just as the trade union leaders in Britain at the present time seek to influence both Conservative and Labour government indiscriminately, although obviously expecting to achieve more from the latter than the former, so the American union leaders lobby Democrats and Republicans without distinction, in spite of a well-founded conviction that the former are more favourably disposed to their point of view than the latter. The 'logic' of pressure group activity entails the understanding that no matter what the political philosophy of the government of the day, it may nevertheless be moved to action in a desired direction, provided that the pressure group in question looks capable of mobilizing a substantial body of voters behind its intentions. What trade unions represent to the American politician are organizations determined to ensure that their members are properly registered and got to the polls on election day, that they are made aware of which candidates are friends and which enemies to their economic interests, and that pamphlets and other literature about election issues are widely distributed, and radio and television programmes adequately sponsored. Of course, the trade unions in America are not linked to the Democratic Party in the way in which British trade unions are linked to the Labour Party —by affiliation—so that they take no part in its policy deliberations, but they have been known to issue the threat of creating their own political party to demonstrate that they are seriously politically involved, and to swing reluctant Democrats around to supporting policies which they approve. So long as they can continue effectively to persuade politicians in the existing Parties to work for their admittedly limited objectives, the trade union leaders see no special benefit in founding a political party which would do no more than this.

In this connection it should also be emphasized that a central focus of united trade union endeavour at Washington is relatively recent. Unlike the T.U.C., which has a record of unbroken existence and progressive growth as a political force since 1868, there has been no unified action in America until latterly because the trade union movement has been internally divided by controversies over both political and industrial issues throughout its history (Morris, 1958, Taft, 1959). The American Federation of Labour, for example, was originally founded in 1886 with the promise that it would act in America very much in the way in which the T.U.C. was acting in Britain. Its constitution drew attention to the conflict between the capitalist as oppressor and the labourer as oppressed, and its first meeting urged 'a most generous support' for an 'independent political movement of the working man' (Taft, 1957). In the 1890's American Federation of Labour conventions passed many Labour Party type resolutions, calling for compulsory education, an eight-hour day, sanitary inspection of workplaces and homes, employers' liability for accidents, municipal ownership of public transport, gas and electricity, and the nationalization of the telegraph service, the railways and the mines (Karson, 1958). At the same time the unions, under the guidance of the American Federation of Labour, were concerned to perfect a militant, collective-bargaining instrument, most successfully amongst craftsmen, and this concern overshadowed more radical political objectives. Thus, although the American Federation of Labour never ceased to be active as a pressure group, it became relatively quiescent in politics—to such an extent in fact that, in the Depression Years, when many new unions were established among the semi-skilled workers of the mass-production industries (Derber & Young, 1957), a number of union leaders split away from the American Federation of Labour to form a new federation, the Congress of Industrial Organizations, pledged *inter alia* to support the New Deal administration and to press for legislation for welfare purposes (Morris, 1958).

The eventual merger of these two bodies in 1955 should not obscure the important points that for twenty years trade union leaders were unable to act in concert over either industrial or political issues and that therefore the likelihood of the trade union movement creating, or supporting the creation of, a third political party in such a circumstance was small. The nature of the American political system also set a limitation on what the more politically militant trade unionists might fruitfully attempt. Since each of the 48 States, as well as Congress, passes its own legislation, a political challenge to the existing parties must necessarily be mounted on a very wide, and expensive, front. This constitutional constraint has not, of course, been changed since the formation of the A.F.L.-C.I.O. in 1955, and it no doubt continues to cause trade union leaders to hesitate about forming a political party to represent labour's aims, although there is clear evidence that legislation and administration of the economy by the government has become more important in union strategy in recent times, directing the attention of the government much more pointedly to welfare problems (Barbash, 1963). As President Johnson put it in 1969, over the education of the young, medical assistance for the old, and the conservation of human and natural resources, no single group 'has been more responsible for the advances in this field in the last five years than the A.F.L.-C.I.O. headed by George Meany' (quoted in Barbash, 1972).

This very recent support by American trade union leaders for government intervention with welfare objectives in mind draws attention to another striking feature of traditional business unionism which is on the wane, namely, the belief in the capacity of American industry to meet the demands of the trade unions. One of the reasons why welfare policies to be implemented by legislation were not popular in the past amongst trade unionists was the relative ease with which so-called 'fringe' benefits could be won from some employers. Collective bargaining in America has embraced not only wages and conditions of work but employer payments into employee pension and supplementary unemployment benefit schemes, and into health and welfare funds which insure wage earners against death, disability, and non-occupational sickness and accidents. Some of the energy which might have gone into pressure group politics working for national welfare services provided by the state out of taxation, has been directed to making such services a charge on industry itself, a feature of the American economy which has more in common with Russia than with Britain. Of course, the rise of the welfare state here has coincided with fifty years or so of relative economic decline, suggesting that British employers could probably not have met a demand for welfare through collective bargaining, had the trade unions made it; and it has only very recently become apparent in America that private welfare schemes leave many people unprotected and foster the illusion that the system is adequate (Wilensky, 1965). Whereas the British intention has been to provide services nationally and universally, the American alternative has covered, at best, only those workers for whom collective bargaining was already the established mode for dealing with employers and, at worst, only a small proportion of these. In 1957, for example, no more than about 40% of American workers were covered by fringe benefits of any kind, that is, including payment for holidays, sick leave, absence from the job by shop-stewards, etc. in addition to the more broadly conceived welfare schemes referred to above (Ulman, 1961). American experience, indeed, indicates that a trade union movement which attempts to innovate socially through collective bargaining alone can achieve but limited success. From this point of view the pursuit of 'causes' by the leaders of the A.F.L.-C.I.O. may be interpreted as belated awareness amongst them that there are many essential services in a modern society which cannot be provided by voluntary effort but must be enforced by the state or one of its agencies.

This interpretation, to be sure, turns on the assumption that business unionism in America has always implied more than the single-minded pursuit of the economic interests of the individual trade union member and that its pressure group activities in Washington, together with collective bargaining for fringe benefits, represent not a form of capitalism for the proletariat, as this term might ordinarily be understood (Bell, 1958), but rather a special kind of collectivist challenge to un-regulated individualism. The study of business unionism, that is to say, brings out a feature of trade unionism as a social movement which is much less obvious in those countries where trade union leaders have regularly expressed their objectives in terms of anti-capitalism as such. What trade unionism primarily represents is a rejection of the theory of economic individualism, characteristic of the capitalist epoch in its classical phase. Such a theory held, on the one hand, that the man with capital might deploy his resources as he thought fit, employing and dismissing workers from his employment according to the nature of the market for their products and his judgement of their skills, capacities, and general willingness to carry out his orders at work, and on the other hand, that the man without capital, hired by the hour or by the day, would be free to leave his job on his own decision, whenever these conditions became no longer acceptable or whenever better terms of employment were offered elsewhere. According to this theory the employer could not be held to be responsible for or to his employees, and equally they could not be held to be responsible for or to him. In the workplace and in the market everyone was responsible for no-one and to no-one but himself. Thus, competition between workers for the best advantage they could obtain was as much a creed of economic individualism as competition between capitalists.

The formation of a trade union challenges this creed in the market for labour by substituting collective for individual bargaining between employer and employee, just as the formation of a joint-stock company, a Trust, a cartel, a merger— oligopolies and monopolies generally—challenges it in this and other markets by substituting collective for individual bargaining between buyers and sellers generally. The essential characteristic of both these challenges is the same, to increase the economic advantage of those who favour collective action by reducing competition between them, and this implies that they have roughly the same skills, goods or services to offer. The rejection of economic individualism does not mean that the advocates of some kind of collective action necessarily have egalitarianism as an objective; and it is a striking feature of trade unionism that for all its emphasis on the democratic control of the trade unions—one man, one vote—it has steadfastly maintained a policy of differentials in income—the rate for the job—a notion that there is in some sense a proper hierarchy of incomes which reflects differences between people in the relative value of the work they do (Wootton, 1955).

Business unionism is a form of trade unionism which clearly holds to such differentiation as the basis of its organizing and economic creeds. Quite apart from rivalries between unions over who should organize whom about what, some trade unions in America have long histories of discrimination against minorities, especially negroes, which the A.F. of L., the C.I.O. and the A.F.L.-C.I.O. have only been partially successful in combating (Marshall, 1965). Such discrimination is, of course, quite in accord with the desire to reduce competition between workers for jobs by limiting the access of whole categories of people to such jobs, since it is consistent with the notion of a hierarchy of incomes for work actually done, as apposed to a first reference to the capacities, or potentialities, of people who might do this work.

The question at issue, therefore, is how it is possible for the A.F.L.-C.I.O. leaders to pursue causes when so many of their member unions are purely interest oriented. The answer lies in the nature of the causes pursued. A programme of education for the young and welfare for the old concentrates on people who have not yet entered or have altogether left the labour market. Action on their behalf does not obviously impinge upon the notion of a hierarchy of incomes for jobs. Nor, granted that collective bargaining will continue to be pursued for fringe benefits, may the demand for services for the unemployed or the sick, to be provided out of taxation, necessarily conflict with the business union conception of collective endeavour, provided that these are not on so lavish a scale as to undermine the differential advantages of those in strong and wealthy unions. The A.F.L.-C.I.O. leaders who sit on government advisory committees and mix with senators and civil servants in Washington may continue to work for welfare objectives of this nature without much hindrance from their fellow trade unionists, because they are apparently not threatening the more immediate aims of the business union philosophy. But why should they work for them at all, if, as the I.L.O. mission claimed, they demonstrate no questioning of the basis of the American economic and social system? Here the answer seems to be that, irrespective of their private political views, trade union leaders in America, like their counterparts in Europe, cannot avoid being concerned with more general aims of national policy and welfare once they are appointed to serve on such committees and other government agencies. The pursuit of 'business' objectives beyond the field of collective bargaining with employers, into the political arena through pressure group activity has the unanticipated consequence that a more than purely business conception of the trade union function is enjoined of the men at the top of the union hierarchies. The modern industrial state seems perforce to be concerned to provide at least a minimum of welfare services for its citizens and, to the degree that it is so concerned, all who seek to participate in political decision making, whatever their motives, find themselves obliged to accept some responsibility for the decisions they are involved in making. This is why American trade union leaders have become 'cause' oriented, for all that members of their unions continue to put their industrial and collective interests before such causes.

In sociological terms trade unions in America, as in Britain, may nowadays be said to be part of a lobbying system which links them with the political administrative machine in very much the same fashion as they are part of a collective bargaining system which links them with the industrial administrative machine. A diagram, analogous to Diagram 1 on page 21 (above) illustrates the role pattern which this system entails.

COLLECTIVE BARGAINING

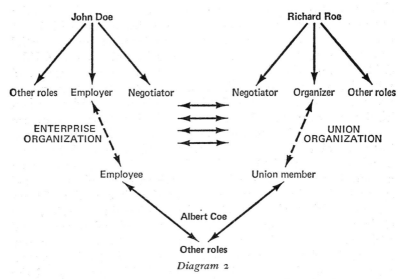

Diagram 2

Two points of clarification are necessary to justify the terminology and symbolism of Diagram 2. In the first place, the use of the term 'legislator' indicates that pressure group activity links the trade union leader, as lobbyist, with politicians and civil servants in their role of law makers, not simply in the sense of passing legislation in the two houses of Congress or the Houses of Parliament, but also in the sense of drafting orders and regulations with the force of law outside these bodies, in the offices of the American President, his aides and officials, or those of the Prime Minister, his Ministerial colleagues and the permanent officials in their Departments. As two American writers have put it, only in the most formal sense can the work of the legislature, properly so-called, be distinguished from that of other parts of government. 'Administrative decisions, often formalized and published as orders and rules, constitute another part of the "law". The contribution of the judiciary to law making includes common law, the interpretation of statutory law, and constitutional law. Moreover, if we define the legislature's task exclusively as law making, how can we explain the fact that most bills are drafted by executive departments or by pressure groups' (Jewell and Patterson, 1966). Indeed, the inclusion in Diagram 2 of two roles, both carried out in this case by the same person—although not necessarily so—helps to clarify the point. In his legislative role, Edward Poe decides what policies to implement in what form, in this instance under pressure from the trade union leader, Richard Roe. In his administrative role, he carries them out, or rather, gives orders to his subordinates to carry them out; and as they are likely in this case to be welfare decisions Albert Coe, as citizen, becomes recipient of benefits accruing from the policy decisions.

In the second place, the set of arrows linking the two hierarchies, trade unions and administrative, draws attention to the fact that 'legislative behaviour takes place at all levels of government—national, state, county, municipal, school district'. (Jewell and Patterson, 1966.) The solid arrow indicates that pressure mostly comes from the trade union national, state, county or municipal representative to the relevant legislature, the President or the State governor, or lesser executive personnel. Insofar as one result of this pressure is for the legislator to invite the lobbyist on to a committee or in other ways to participate in policy making there is some counter-pressure; but as this is not a reciprocal process, in the sense that there is reciprocity between trade union and enterprise representatives as 'negotiators' in the collective bargaining system, it is designated here by the broken arrow. Trade union lobbyists and legislators do not bargain, nor do they negotiate as a general rule, over the issues for which trade unionists have entered the lobbies. Nevertheless, there is an element of inverse correspondence in their relationship which consists in the legislator trying to persuade the lobbyist to look beyond the immediate issue to the more general responsibility of the legislator for national purposes.

This draws attention to the matter raised at the end of Chapter IV (above, page 47), namely, a possible explanation for the rise to importance of the role of shop steward lying in the trade union emphasis on changing the economic system towards one more responsive to the requirements of individual workers. From the individual trade union member's point of view, whether he be primarily interested in the unions as a business organization or as part of a social movement, the whole point of engaging in pressure group activity is that it should in some obvious way be relevant to the solution of problems on the shop floor. This does not mean that he will automatically be opposed to a concentration on national welfare or national policy or even that he believes that if his leaders become too involved in these matters they will neglect more immediate trade union issues; but it does mean that he conceives of the union as a pressuring organization in every sense. Not only in lobbying, but in collective bargaining negotiations, the trade union representative is usually the initiator. Hence the shop steward has emerged in recent times as the effective local officer to begin such negotiations, some of which are not about wages but about the same kinds of issue locally as engage the lobbyist in politics nationally —the general welfare of the citizens, the general welfare of the worker as citizen. Because the trade union has become a powerful pressure group in politics its local representatives have become recognized as capable of wielding some of this power in the economic system, and because the conception of a trade union is that it is a democratic organization of members, members believe that the shop steward should apply this pressure locally just as their leaders apply it nationally, although not in the political but directly in the employing organization. Of course, all this turns on the assumption that leaders and rank-and-file members think alike on these issues and that there is agreement on the pursuit of trade union objectives everywhere by all representatives equally. By contrast, some authors believe that there is now such a divergence in outlook between leaders who have become part of the legislative hierarchy and shop floor members who are subject to its decisions that the very nature of trade union democracy has been changed. The leaders are nowadays the masters rather than the servants of the members. How far this is true is the subject matter of the last part of this book.

PART 3:

Instrument of
Democratic Participation

CHAPTER VIII

The Sociology of Democratic Organization

The *problem* of democratic organization, summed up by Michels in a famous phrase—'who says organization, says oligarchy'—was first expressed by the Webbs in their analysis of changes in the structure of trade union government. 'In passing from a local to a national organization,' they wrote, 'the Trade Union unwittingly left behind the ideal of primitive democracy. The setting apart of one man to do the clerical work destroyed the possibility of equal and identical service by all the members, and laid the foundation of a separate governing class. The practice of requiring members to act in rotation was silently abandoned. Once chosen for his post, the general secretary could rely with confidence, unless he proved himself obviously unfit or grossly incompetent, on being annually re-elected. Spending all day at office work, he soon acquired a professional expertness quite out of the reach of his fellow-members at the bench or the forge. And even if some other member possessed natural gifts equal or superior to the acquired skill of the existing officer, there was, in a national organization, no opportunity of making these qualities known.' (S. and B. Webb, 1898.)

Two different, although related, aspects of change in the circumstances of trade union are emphasized in this analysis:

(1) the necessity for trade union government to pass from primitive to some other form of democracy as the number of members grew beyond the possibility of them all being personally acquainted with one another and as these numbers inevitably were dispersed over a wider geographical area, and

(2) the necessity for the administration of trade union affairs to

become an increasingly efficient and powerful instrument of collective bargaining and of social change.

In a system of primitive democracy *all* the members of the organization *can*, and often do, meet together to make rules and regulations and to decide how they are to be applied to particular cases, agree what to do about raising money and spending it, and generally both make policy and apply it to issues as they arise. By 1892, however, the average size of trade unions in the United Kingdom was already 1,280 members, a figure which had grown to 13,820 by 1952 (Roberts, 1956). Clearly some unions might still be small enough, even in 1952, for primitive democracy to be possible, but the largest were already too large for all their members to assemble in one place for debates in which all, or at least most, voices could be heard. Some other form of union government had to be invented.

The Webbs, indeed, discussed a number of devices which were tried by trade unions in an attempt to maintain the quality of primitiveness—the referendum, the initiative, the delegation —and concluded that all these, together with rotation of office and the mass meeting, led 'straight either to inefficiency and disintegration, or to the uncontrolled dominance of a personal dictator or an expert bureaucracy.... The old theory of democracy is still an article of faith, and constantly comes to the front when any organization has to be formed for brand-new purposes; but Trade Union constitutions have undergone a silent revolution'. To replace the primitive assembly there had emerged 'the typically modern form of democracy, the elected representative assembly, appointing and controlling an executive committee under whose direction the permanent official staff performs its work'. (S. and B. Webb, 1898.) Insofar as the desire to make the trade union a more powerful participant in industrial relations and in pressure group politics led its members to seek strength through numbers and to prefer efficiency in operations, representative democracy was the best device they could find for still providing some avenues whereby rank-and-file members might continue to play a part in the conduct of union affairs.

Side by side with the transformation of the trade union from a primitive to a representative democracy there also occurred, for largely the same reason, a transmutation in its manner of implementing its decisions from accomplishment by amateurs to administration by professionals. Initially, the business of a union was conducted by ordinary members in their spare time, serving in rotation or as elected delegates whose term of office was deliberatively and strictly limited. The appointment of a General Secretary and his gradual reinforcement by a staff of national, regional and divisional organizers, research officers and other office personnel, all full-time employees of the union, were in one sense no more than a further example of the increasing division of labour which seems to result inevitably from an expansion in the scale of operations, but in another, it led to problems of democratic control, altogether different from those raised by the advent of representative union government. These administrative roles are specialisms, requiring skills which have to be developed, often through years of experience in administration. The rank-and-file trade unionist does not possess these skills and may only dimly appreciate their significance because the nature of his everyday occupation in manual or routine clerical work provides him with no opportunity to learn even the rudiments of such expertise. The problem of democratic organization, that is to say, turns on the extent to which the many can continue to govern the few, when the role of the trade union member and those of the various officers who act on his behalf become so differentiated and separated by intermediaries that direct communication no longer seems possible and the effort to bridge the gap seems beyond the imagination of the leaders, on the one hand, and the rank-and-file on the other.

This manner of presenting the problem, to be sure, gives it a rather different appearance from that given it by those writers on the internal government of trade unions who have taken their point of departure from Michels' study of oligarchic tendencies in democratic political parties. Thus Lipset and his colleagues have expressed themselves in terms of an 'entrenched' oligarchy and the 'impossibility' of dislodging leaders from office because such men have 'overwhelming power', wish to stay in office, and 'will adopt dictational tactics to do so'. Looking at Michels' formulation as an undoubted 'iron law' these authors have convinced themselves that there is 'no more persuasive illustration of the unanticipated consequence of men's purposeful social action than the recurrent transformations of nominally democratic private organizations into oligarchies more concerned with preserving and enhancing their own power and status than in satisfying the demands and interests of the members' (Lipset, *et al.*, 1956). Misunderstanding, suspicion and overt hostility on all sides are, of course, unanticipated consequences of the departure from primitive democracy and amateurism in the name of more effective, purposeful trade union action, but to describe the trade union as inevitably oligarchic implies that the device of representative democracy has no power to check the drift in this direction which the professionalization of administration might otherwise produce. The choice for study of a 'two-party' system in the International Typographical Union of America, indeed, by its very rarity and fortuitous existence, must lead to the pessimistic conclusion that there is an absence of democracy in trade unions (Lipset, *et al.*, 1956). The alternative, a comparative approach to the study of large-scale democratic organizations, requires a closer look at the device of representative government in such bodies.

The chief feature of significance to notice is the distinction between the delegate and the representative. Under a system of primitive democracy all decisions are made at a meeting of members. Hence when they elect one of their number to speak or act on their behalf elsewhere they choose him as a delegate, that is, one whose duties are to vote *only* according to their instructions and to propose *only* those measures which they have themselves already discussed and decided upon. What the Webbs called the 'Imperative Mandate' (S. and B. Webb, 1898) was a device to confine decision-making to the localities since no decisions might properly be made at a delegate meeting unless they had already been concluded at the meetings which elected the delegates and instructed them. An elected *representative*, by contrast, is empowered to speak and vote for those who elect him without the constraint of such a mandate. This means that he may be as much influenced in his decision-making by the views of other representatives at the assembly as by those of the people who have elected him to represent them there. The crucial issue, however, is that he must report back to them to explain why he chose to act in the way he did rather than in the way they might have expected, and he may be severely reprimanded if they are not persuaded that he has represented them adequately. There is, it should be understood, nothing they can do at this stage about the decision that has been made but on some future occasion they can send some other person who might better represent their point of view or trust that the former representative now understands more clearly what he should do. In a system of delegation democracy operates to determine projects. In a system of representation it judges by results. The control of the union leader in such a system works by reference to what he has already done, not by deciding what he has to do.

Of course, a modern trade union is a complex mixture of delegation, representation and outright appointment. To the outsider there is 'a bewildering variety of organizational arrangements' between the rank-and-file member and the national leaders (Mills, 1948), but the conception of representative democracy which generally pervades these arrangements entails that at every level the behaviour of an officer, or an official, is open to challenge publicly by a representative on the ground that it does not accord with what he thinks is best, either for the union as a whole or for that part of it which he represents. Would-be oligarchs in trade unions face this 'iron law of democracy', so that it is in open debate with representatives, rather than through manipulation of written communications with the rank and file, that they must seek to perpetuate their personal authority. Lipset and his colleagues placed much emphasis on 'the permanent tenure in office' of union leaders and argued that democracy 'implies permanent insecurity for those in governing positions: the more truly democratic the governing system, the greater the insecurity', from which they concluded, by definition, that trade unions were not democratic. In this conclusion they ignored the extent to which trade union leaders maintain themselves in office in spite of being obliged regularly to meet representatives from all sections of their union and to justify their performance to them. The permanence of their tenure is a consequence of their ability to win over enough of their critics to their own point of view and not a cause of their power to stifle opposition.

In part Lipset and his colleagues recognized this fact, since they pointed to the *political* skills of 'the administration' and

contrasted these with 'the absence of these skills among the rank
and file.... The union official, to maintain his position, must
become adept in political skills. The average worker, on the
other hand, has little opportunity or need to acquire them'
(Lipset, *et al.*, 1956). Curiously enough, these authors did not
explain why it was that union leaders *must* develop them when
'the only viewpoints about union matters that are widely available to the members are those of the administration'. What they
have apparently failed to appreciate is that representative
democracy works on the principle that between the rank-and-
file member and the top men there are very many aspiring
leaders whose challenge must be met and whose political skills
are not negligible. A proper study of the mechanisms of representative democracy must include an investigation of the part
played by district, regional and national assemblies in the
development of such skills amongst the erstwhile rank and file.

In his study of 'proletarian' political parties Michels drew
attention to the greatly superior education which had been re-
ceived by the leaders as compared with the members and suggested that this was a further aspect of the oligarchic tendencies
in modern democracies. Lipset and his colleagues did not refer
to this as a possibility in trade unions, although an earlier study
had drawn a contrast between the leaders of the A.F. of L. and
the C.I.O. and the United States adult population. Whereas only
24% of the last had gone through high school or beyond, 39% of
the leaders of the A.F. of L. and 56% of those of the C.I.O. had
graduated from high school or gone to college—more, indeed,
had gone to college from high school than had not. Between the
two bodies, moreover, the striking difference was that the older,
national leaders of the A.F. of L. were not so highly educated
as the younger, local leaders, while in the C.I.O., the much more
recently established organization, the reverse was the case (Mills,
1948). Can such educational differences be interpreted to mean
that more formal schooling gives men an advantage in learning
those political skills which will provide opportunities for leadership, especially in those unions which are composed of the semi-
skilled and the unskilled workers?

Such questions are not easily answered, although what little
evidence we have indicates that the anti-intellectual ideology
pervading the trade union movement, with its superior evalua-

tion of practical experience as opposed to theoretical facility, tends to prevent the formally educated as such from playing much part in trade union affairs, save in subsidiary roles to the elected leadership. In recent times American trade unions have increasingly employed university graduates as experts in research posts, for editing union journals and as contact men with government departments. These experts, it should be emphasized, are appointed, not elected. They are responsible directly to the union leaders, who have been given powers to appoint and dismiss them as they see fit (Leiserson, 1959), subject to whatever accounting they must make in this respect to the representative body. A study of this type of expert in his relation to the union leader has reported that he 'typically has consistent, sustained, high influence on problems that the top officers see as far from the core function of their union', most notably 'in the areas of public relations and relations with government'. These are typically areas where direct experience of work on the factory floor is not seen to be relevant, although, indeed, those men who can combine such experience with some technical knowledge are more likely to be influential than those without it, not excluding the 'synthetic rank-and-filer', the graduate who spends a short period in a factory to obtain 'a brief identification as a wage worker' (Wilensky, 1956). If formal education conveys any advantage it does so when it is not at all obvious.

In brief, the transmutation of trade union management by amateurs into administration by professionals has not taken place through the appointment of a bureaucracy of experts, although this has also occurred. What has happened is that this bureaucracy has been created *to serve* elected representatives whose professional skill derives from a different source from that which has produced the expert. The full-time leader gets to the top of the union representative hierarchy only after many years of service in the representative not the bureaucratic hierarchy (Roberts, 1956). As a general rule he starts on the shop floor and through his experience as a shop-steward, a collector of subscriptions, a union branch secretary, begins to administer local union affairs on an unpaid amateurish basis before eventually becoming a part-time and then a full-time officer. Education may well be important but only insofar as it helps men to perform adequately in these roles. It is in consequence of this performance, not by virtue of their education, that men get selected for union advancement. The expert, by contrast, is appointed precisely because he is educated and before anything is known about his performance in union work.

This discussion of representative democracy clearly indicates that the theory of oligarchic tendencies in trade unions is unsubstantiated by the facts. The union leadership at all levels is regularly challenged by the members responsible for democratic decisions, including the election of officers, at these levels. Nevertheless, although the reference to the great gulf between the union leader and the rank-and-file member may not be used to substantiate such a theory of oligarchy, it has sufficient force to raise the possibility that what has occurred in the departure from primitive democracy has been the creation of what has been called a 'polyarchy', a balance of power between the leaders and a minority of *active* participants. 'The larger and the more active this group,' it has been suggested, 'the closer the organization approaches the ideal of the democratic theorists. The smaller its number and strength, the more the organization moves towards the oligarchic pole' (van de Vall, 1970). Since the concept of representative democracy holds out the possibility that all the members may participate only at the very bottom of the hierarchy, trade unions must be, by definition, polyarchies, except where participation at this level is so intense that every officer above is continuously made aware of rank-and-file demands. The crucial issues for trade union democracy, that is to say, turn on the nature of participation at this level and on the quality of the interpretations which the active participants make about the attitudes and opinions, needs and interests of the passive rank and file.

The most obvious approach to the first of these issues has been to estimate the amount of participation at local union meetings in terms of the proportion of members attending. Unfortunately, trade union clubs, branches or locals vary in size from less than one hundred members on the roll to over ten thousand (Roberts, 1956). The range of proportions in attendance may thus reflect as much the way in which branch membership is divided within a union as it indicates the level of participation within those branches. More illuminating, therefore, have been those studies which have reported on the kinds of decision which are made at branch meetings, as related to participation, such as that attendance rises when the union is in open conflict with employers (Dean, 1954a) and that the importance of decisions varies when they are made in small as compared with large branches (Strauss and Sayles, 1953a), or that decision-making is concentrated higher up in the union hierachy when branches are scattered as compared with where they are closer together, geographically speaking (Raphael, 1965). However, a more general criticism that can be made of the use of membership participation as an index of democracy is that it rests on the assumption that all trade union members have, or should have, the same basic reasons for participating. Yet interviews with rank-and-file unionists in America have regularly uncovered significant differences between them in their attitudes to the union and to their employers, leading to the plausible conclusion that they may be classified into distinct types, ranging from the 'ideological' trade unionist, through the 'good' union man, the loyal but critical member, the crisis activist, the dually oriented member, the card carrier or indifferent member, to the unwilling unionist (Tagliacozzo and Seidman, 1956). The study of participation *as fact*, that is to say, can ill afford to ignore the effect of personality and other differences in people and their circumstances which influence the likelihood of their filling participatory roles. A democratic system of government is one which has been designed to eliminate institutional barriers which might otherwise prevent members from expressing their opinions and in other ways participating. It is not apparently one which results in all the members in the system having the same or equal motives for so behaving.

The term 'dually oriented member' in the above typology is used to draw attention to the trade unionist whose allegiance to his union is only marginally greater than indifferent and who considers the pursuit of his personal interests to lie as much outside the province of trade unionism as within it. He is, indeed, the worker who thinks his chances of rising to supervisory level in his employment to be good and who, therefore, expects to give up his union membership before long. Dual orientation should not be confused with the term 'dual loyalty' which is often used in American literature on trade unionism and which refers to 'good' union men and critical loyalists who accompany strong union support with an equally positive attitude to their employers, even when open conflict occurs between the latter and their union (Purcell, 1953; Dean, 1954b). The recognition that some union members are dually loyal in these respects, while others are active only in crises, or are dually oriented, indifferent and unwilling unionists raises the question of whether it is possible for the union activists to make an accurate interpretation of the range of attitudes and opinions, needs and interests of the various types of member who form the branches in which they are active. If by democracy it is understood that all these points of view are to be reflected in the processes of decision-making—as they might well be where a system of primitive democracy prevails—the representatives of the branches, as well as the activists within them, must surely pay them as much attention as they give to their own partisan viewpoints, 'partisan' because the mere fact of being active presupposes supporting at least one facet of the 'ideological' position, namely, that the trade union is both an instrument of collective bargaining and an instrument of social change. The alternative conception, that trade unions are not democracies in this sense but polyarchies, stresses the extent to which the activists do not attempt to represent member opinions but instead engage in a contest with other activists over what collective bargaining and the trade union movement generally may be used to achieve. The element of democracy that prevails in this lies in the obvious fact that any member may participate in this contest if he is prepared to attend the meetings or take other action to make his opinions heard.

In an earlier chapter it was suggested that in recent times the shop steward has become a link man between the rank-and-file employee and the management of the enterprise which employs him as worker. In the polyarchic system he may also be seen as a link man between the member and the trade union officer. One of the reasons, indeed, why participation in trade union branch meetings has declined is that union members have much easier access to the shop-steward at their place of work than they have to their branch secretary, unless he happens also to be working there. They are able, that is to say, to express grievances and be critical about the firm *and the union* to the steward at work without making use of the formal machinery of union government, and just as managers prefer to negotiate with shop stewards rather than with union officials, so union members prefer to 'participate' through their shop stewards rather than approach the union hierachy. Of course, shop stewards vary in their effectiveness as link men in this respect and in the degree to which trade union officers are able to use them in return to communicate with members who do not bother to go to meetings. American shop stewards, indeed, have been said to be of three types—the social worker, the politician cum organizer-policeman, and the self seeker (Sayles and Strauss, 1953)—and these differences in orientation on their part will undoubtedly show themselves in differences in the way in which the role of steward is carried out. Nevertheless, the general point remains that in addition to the factors within the enterprise which have led to the need for a shop steward in the industrial relations system, there are factors within the organization of a modern, large scale trade union which have led to the need for the shop steward within a democracy. How this operates in detail will be considered in the next two chapters.

CHAPTER IX

Union Democracy in Britain

Once trade union branches began to grow in membership beyond the capacity of a branch secretary to keep in touch with actual and potential members, the need for someone in each workplace to accept responsibility for recruiting new employees and collecting union subscriptions became increasingly apparent. It was not long after this point that 'stewards' became involved in negotiations and other union functions in their place of work. Thus, by the 1890's it had become accepted practice with the National Amalgamated Union of Labour, one of the new, general unions, 'for the official delegate to take the shop steward into the "office" with him when he went to talk to the employer' (Clegg, 1964). The particular knowledge of local conditions possessed by shop stewards, gave them a very special place in the collective bargaining process which the officers of the trade unions soon recognized and utilized in their negotiations with employers. What was not so immediately obvious to them was that this particular knowledge of workshop conditions also included a particular knowledge of the wishes, expectations and, indeed, idiosyncrasies of workshop members and that therefore the shop steward might well fill a very special place in the democratic processes of trade union government. Once primitive democracy had given way to representative democracy and branches had grown so large that only a relatively small proportion of union members attended branch meetings, the point of view of the rank-and-file member in the workshop could not be heard without a representative of the shop to speak on his behalf.

The significance of the role of shop steward in this respect emerged quite dramatically in this country during the First World War. In 1915 the government and the trade unions signed a Treasury agreement whereby the latter pledged them-selves to an industrial truce for the duration of the war on the understanding that the government would fully restore trade union rights at the end of hostilities. They also agreed to allow the greater use of unskilled and semi-skilled labour in factories engaged directly on war work on the condition that profits accru-ing to employers from such 'dilution' of skill would be limited by the government. What was not apparently foreseen was that dilution would create a very large number of workshop prob-lems which could not be dealt with effectively save by workers familiar with worshop practices. Within a few years unions and employers were obliged to define the role of shop stewards in these and other negotiations and to come to terms with the newly formed workshop committees, that is, committees of shop stewards organized to co-ordinate the activities of the stewards in the various shops in a workplace.

The government and the trade unions also apparently under-estimated the strength of hostility to dilution on the part of skilled workmen in the engineering industry; and the imple-mentation of the Treasury agreement was followed in some parts of the country by strikes against the employers, against the gov-ernment, and against the leaders of the trade union movement. While it is true that shop stewards were not always completely antagonistic to their union officials over the issue of dilution and that there were many instances of co-operation between them, it is nevertheless the case that for the most part the local organ-izations of shop stewards during the war represented the focus of opposition to the official union policy. For a while, in fact, a shop stewards' 'movement' appeared to be on the verge of con-solidating a national organization to maintain a general strike policy in the name of the rank-and-file and to pursue a campaign for the workers' control of industry as alternatives to the policies pursued by the T.U.C.; but the restitutions of union rights and practices at the end of the war quickly removed the urgency of the need for workshop bargaining, and the workers' committees soon disappeared (Pribićević, 1959). Nevertheless the office of shop steward remained a necessary one in many unions; this in spite of a general development towards national bargaining under the system of Joint Industrial Councils set up by succes-sive post-war governments; and gradually, over the next twenty years, trade union rule books were amended to give formal recognition to the role played by the shop steward in the workplace and in the branch (Goodman and Whittingham, 1969). Thus, from being considered a 'revolutionary' opponent to the union leaders the steward has eventually come to be described in official union handbooks as a grass-roots administrator, communicating union policy to the rank-and-file member and reporting members' views to the branch (McCarthy, 1967).

British experience during the First World War is, however, not altogether irrelevant for an understanding of the actual role played by shop stewards in the democratic process. One persistent consequence of the pursuit of dilution of skill in the engineering industry was an upsurge of strike action, usually on a local basis and wholly unofficial. Since the trade union leaders had signed an agreement with the government to keep an industrial truce in the country's military interest they could not support, nor condone, these strikes. Their recurrence, therefore, may be correctly interpreted as a rejection of official union policy by sections of the rank-and-file (Pribićević, 1959), but this must not be misunderstood. Most strikes at any time seem to originate in the more-or-less spontaneous action of workers at their place of work. They cease to be unofficial only because most of them obtain the official authorization the strikers appeal for (Hyman, 1972). Consequently, a strike which continues in spite of the refusal of the elected trade union officers to give it official backing is an indication of serious disagreement within the union. In other words, the wartime strikers considered their grievances over dilution at the local level to warrant unconstitutional action in spite of the dilemmas of their union leaders *vis-à-vis* the government. These leaders, for their part, were prepared to ignore local grievances in the face of the demand that they give whole-hearted support to the war effort. In a sense this may all be seen as a serious failure of communication within the unions in that neither the rank-and-file members nor the union leaders seemed to be able to appreciate the complexities of each other's situation. Such an interpretation, though, is valid only on the understanding that the shop steward can act as communicator solely in those circumstances where there is already a marked willingness on the part of all parties concerned to consider sympathetically the arguments of their apparent opponents, which in turn implies a substantial area of agreement between them already. Such consensus did not exist in these crucial war years. Although the engineers wanted to win the war, they did not want to win it at any price and they believed the price that their leaders were asking them to pay was too high.

Of course, lacking official leadership these wartime strikes had necessarily to be organized by local leaders and for the most part the shop stewards undertook this task. Indeed, shop stewards to this day have appeared prominent in accounts of unofficial strikes, with the consequence that rather than being seen as improving communications within trade unions they have been described as militants, in the sense of malcontents, troublemakers or agitators (Goodman and Whittingham, 1969; Hyman, 1972). The official T.U.C. view is that every year shop stewards 'are the instruments for settling thousands of problems quickly and suitably. Most of them work loyally under difficulties with personal sacrifice; it is very few who misuse their office' (Trades Union Congress, 1966). Since in this context an unofficial strike is one which is continued against the advice of the Executive Committee of a union, it may be assumed that those who lead them are misusing their office in this sense; and to the degree that the strikers are quite deliberately rejecting the policy of their union as this is expressed by its officers, the misuse of office by shop stewards may be seen as an instance of action by a local minority in contradiction to the interests of the majority. The polyarchic concept of democracy, that is to say, implies that the balance of power within a union produces compromises which are intended to reflect the interests, not of all but nevertheless of most members, and, indeed, the assertion that the great bulk of shop stewards are 'loyal' is an indication of the strength of this conception, since it implies that they accept the compromise even when the members in their shop are disadvantaged. The polyarchic notion, that is to say, implies not only a balance of power but a balance of interests which differ from shop to shop and locality to locality. There is no expectation that every interest will be, or can be satisfied, and it is assumed that the leaders for the time being are leaders simply because they symbolize the dominant interests of the moment within the union. They will be replaced in due course as the spokesmen for other interest groups come to succeed in the electoral processes of the union. Shop stewards who conduct unofficial strikes are thus thought to misuse their office because they are refusing to accept the implications of democracy as it is exemplified in the polyarchic form. Although the local interests of their members do not coincide with the dominant interests pursued by the union, they are nevertheless demanding that they should be satisfied.

Such a view of unofficial strikes is rejected by those whose conception of union democracy is rather more 'primitive'. From their point of view the fact that shop stewards are in immediate, practical touch with the rank-and-file members means that their conduct of such strikes is the expression of an essentially democratic need and not the rejection of it. As one author has put it in the context of inflation since the end of the Second World War, 'the existence in Britain of a high proportion of unofficial strikes indicates an important defect in formal union activity'. Because the day-to-day activities of a trade union official are remote from those of the members in the workshop he has no personal interest in being energetic in the pursuit of any of their interests; and because he has ceased to be militant on their behalf the shop steward must be militant instead (Allen, 1966), even when this brings him into conflict with the Executive Committee of the union. The attitudes of these elected officers, indeed, are assumed to be identical to those of the officials, and coloured like theirs to the point perhaps of complete lack of vision about what the members' interests are in their desire to maintain a particular image of their union in the eyes of employers, politicians, government officials and officers of organizations like the I.L.O. The institutionalization of collective bargaining and the participation of trade union leaders in the policy-forming committees of the welfare state have given all kinds of trade union leaders a vested interest in maintaining the constitutional forms of decision-making within their union in spite of the fact that only a small minority of members ever made use of it. Local leaders who reject the constitutional forms may therefore be inferred to be grass-roots democrats in the primitive sense of this term.

Detailed evidence on the dynamics of unofficial strikes does not, however, simply confirm this alternative view of trade union democracy. Rather does it suggest that the shop stewards engaged in them are expressing the view of a militant *minority* of the movement. The 1970 Pilkington strike, for example, 'began with only minority support amongst the rank-and-file and it was prolonged for seven weeks despite the wishes of a majority of the strikers to have it called off earlier' (Lane and Roberts, 1971). Although it is clear that in many cases of unofficial action the tempers of members locally are inflamed by what they see as dilatoriness in the operation of constitutional procedures, so that they are prepared to support the local militants in their attempts to speed up the settlement of a dispute in their favour, there is no indication that they prefer this method to the constitutional one, or see their action as symbolic of an alternative form of democracy. This is not to deny that the men involved in an unofficial strike may sometimes have a genuine grievance and that the union leaders are mistaken when they fail to make such strikes official; but this is not at all the same argument as the claim that *therefore* unofficial strikes are a more genuine form of grass-roots 'participation' than attendance at branch and other meetings, and than casting a vote for preferred candidates at elections for higher union officers. No doubt the increase in such strikes in an inflationary situation might suggest to trade union leaders that their short-term achievements are less successful than their long-term results, but as most settlement of disputes occurs without strike action, it is difficult for them, as for many other members of their union, to believe that there can be anything *radically* wrong with the existing machinery for democratic control, however polyarchic it may be.

Shop stewards, of course, regularly hold meetings with their union members at work. They are also much more likely than these members to attend branch meetings and to hold branch office, so that they have become the main means whereby the views of men on the shop floor are conveyed to a wider audience within the union. In many British unions it is also customary for local full-time officers to hold regular meetings with stewards (McCarthy and Parker, 1968). In this way rank-and-file views may bypass the branch and go directly to the union's permanent staff. In any case, the district committees responsible for the work of this staff locally are elected from the branches and may contain shop stewards amongst their members (Roberts,

1956). There are, that is to say, many different ways for shop stewards to participate in the day-to-day conduct of trade unionism and to represent their members at different levels. In the process they meet other views and opinions and, in particular, listen to the demands of shop stewards from other places that *their* members be given priority. The awareness that a trade union is a polyarchy is a recognition that shop stewards who are active in this sense are active, and conscious of participating, in a process of balancing interests one against another. This means that they place their own shop in the context of general union policy and this is why there are in fact so few unofficial strikes, although there are so many shop stewards.

In an earlier chapter it was pointed out that the regular meetings of T.U.C. leaders with representatives of employers and union leaders from other countries at Conference of the I.L.O. take them into realms of experience far beyond those of the rank-and file members of a trade union, and the question was raised whether participation of this kind has resulted in such a divergence of outlook between the leaders and the members that union democracy has been endangered. Clearly, it does require an extraordinary leap of the imagination for an ordinary shop floor worker who never attends any kind of meeting outside his workplace to appreciate the effect of these international encounters on a trade union leader's perception of his role; yet it does not follow from this that the latter has no appreciation of what it is like to be a shop floor worker. While it is true that on average the general secretaries of British unions have spent some twenty years of their lives in some kind of union office before reaching the top (Roberts, 1956) and that therefore their personal experience of routine manual or clerical work is at worst a dim memory and at best a clear recall of events which took place when they were much younger and their world a different place, it is nevertheless true that the act of imagination required to bridge this gap is very much less, assisted as it is by the information provided by today's shop stewards and today's local officers. Where, indeed, the trade union leader is likely to go astray is in failing to apprehend that the ordinary union member sees the union and its purposes so differently from him. To get to the top of a union a man has to become a persuasive debater and an effective organizer and the men he relies on for information in the union have also developed, or are in the process of developing, such skills. They cannot begin to do this until in one sense or another, at one level or another, they have first made themselves responsible for the expenditure of union funds and have represented their union in bargaining with employers (Clegg, Killick and Adams, 1961). When he is talking to fellow trade unionist, the union leader assumes he is talking to someone who thinks about the union in much the same way as he does himself. It is very much more difficult for him to put himself in the place of a member who will accept no responsibilities beyond the payment of union dues which he will in any case neglect to pay if no one calls upon him to collect them, who thinks of union business solely in terms of the settlement of those grievances which arise in *his* place of work.

A trade union leader is often intellectually aware that many trade unionists are no more than card-carrying members, but he does not usually appreciate emotionally the significance of this for the conduct of his union's business and his own place within the union. Because he has been successful in his career and through several elections on his way to the top, he is apt to assume that he represents a majority of members rather than the minority group which dominates at the moment, and in this assumption he is likely to conclude that any opposition to his point of view must of necessity represent an insignificant, if not a misguided or sinister minority, seeking by foul rather than fair means to circumvent the majority. He cannot see it, that is to say, as the expression of how the balance of power works in a polyarchy, in which the great bulk of members have no wish to assume the responsibilities which the concept of democracy as government by the people implies; and this means that in fact the processes of collective bargaining and the pursuit of social reform are carried on by an elite—a minority of members who are in a sense qualitatively different from the majority by virtue of their very willingness to undertake what the latter see as too difficult, too thankless, or too distasteful a task (Banks, 1970).

The recognition that the activities of trade unions are accomplished by an elite goes some way to explaining how it comes about in Britain that a disproportionate number of militant, political activists, especially Communists, are to be found holding union office. 'Communists want to get elected; most trade unionists don't.' (Ferris, 1972.) Communists get elected and continue to get elected, that is to say, not because of their politics but because of their single-minded drive to cope with the drudgery and unpleasantness of union office. A study of the Electrical Trades Union, for example, during the period when it was apparently 'controlled' by the Communist Party has concluded that its Communist leaders were 'as much symptomatic of the union's militant policy as that they themselves were the direct cause of it'. On purely Communist policy issues they were, in fact, regularly defeated at annual conference (Bean, 1965). The E.T.U. case, indeed, is striking not for its Communist 'subversive' implications but for the evidence it presents of the possibilities for any resolute minority to obtain temporary control of elections in a union, if it is prepared to be not only resolute but unscrupulous in the sense that it will falsify results and in other ways ensure that its opponents do not get as equal a chance of election as its protagonists or supporters (Rolph, 1962). It is also clear that unions differ in the nature of their electoral processes and the opportunities they give for ballot-rigging and disputing the results (Edelstein, 1964-5 and 1968). There are thus differences between unions in this country and between those in this country and the U.S.A. in these respects (Edelstein, *et al.*, 1970), and no doubt the variations are worldwide. The main point to notice, however, is that the concept of an elite in this context does not carry any connotation of superior moral or intellectual qualities. The 'superiority' of the elite rests in its capacity for absorbing the tasks which the conduct of a large trade union implies without any judgment about the worthiness of the way this capacity is employed. The fact that a member of this elite, be he a shop steward or a trade union general secretary, is characteristically different from a card-carrying member is what gives trade union democracy its special features, although this is often obscured in a country where there do not appear any institutional barriers preventing card-carriers from becoming activists. A more obvious example—the case of union democracy in ex-colonial territories—may perhaps clarify the issues involved.

CHAPTER X

Union Organization in British Ex-Colonial Africa

'On first visiting a trade union in Asia or Africa a Westerner is likely to ask himself: Where are the members? Where is the organization? All that he can see is a tiny, scantily equipped office, an officer or two, and possibly a clerk. There seem to be no regular meetings of the membership in a given plant, no shop stewards who might serve as a line of communication with the officers.... The organization appears to be all head and no body.' (Millen, 1963.) In part, the explanation for this lies in the rapidity of growth in the number of trade unions in these countries with the onset of industrialization since the end of the Second World War; many of them are small and poorly organized (Roberts, 1964). In part, it lies in the nature of the industrializing process in these countries. In Africa, for example, there has so far been little attempt to build up a stable labour force. There are relatively few landless workers and the mass of manual employees in some countries are migrants who intend to return to their tribal lands after a short spell of wage employment (Scott, 1966). But in part, also, it arises from the attempt by colonial administrators in these territories before independence to introduce elaborate European type trade unions into communities where most of the workers were still illiterate and did not understand the nature of collective bargaining procedures and the need for financially strong organizations of working men. 'The unions have large paper memberships but only small sections of these regularly pay contributions.' Yet they have full-time, educated leaders, many without any industrial experience whatsoever (Allen, 1971), although these are obviously capable of co-operating adequately with the colonial Labour Departments in their respective countries.

Roberts has identified three types of trade union leader, emerging in the colonial territories of the British Commonwealth:

(1) men who rose from the ranks, of whom very few indeed were ex-manual workers, save amongst dockers, miners, and railwaymen;

(2) outsiders who possessed considerable demagogic powers and used them not to build up powerful democratic organizations but a mass following which would advance their own, personal ambitions; and

(3) intellectuals, often educated in Britain, who were excluded by racial discrimination from government office and saw trade unions as offering scope for their administrative talents (Roberts, 1964).

The importance of literacy and fluency in English cannot be over-emphasized in this connection. Although sometimes illiterate workers have been appointed to union administrative posts, where the mass of union members are illiterate, leaders must perforce be recruited from outside the occupations catered for by a union. Most union activity depends at least on the ability to keep records of membership and financial transactions and to read reports as well as, in this instance, to negotiate verbally with state officials and with employers whose major commercial and government activities are transacted in English. Of course, the transition from a colonial territory into a nation state in these African and Asian lands has been accompanied by some displacement of the imperial language by one of the vernacular tongues, but so long as English firms continue to have economic interests in these countries a knowledge of this particular foreign language will be essential for trade union leaders (Allen, 1971).

This is not the place to examine the processes whereby national movements arose in these colonial territories and successful campaigns for independence were conducted. However, the part played by trade unions in these movements should not be overlooked. Not only were they 'political' in the sense that the social movement element in their composition was much more in evidence than their industrial relations instrumentation, but the emphasis on political unity after independence has sometimes meant that the union leadership has been 'co-opted' by the government (Scott, 1966). The trade unions were thus often 'training schools' for political leadership and administration (Millen, 1963) and where their leaders did not in fact leave industrial relations altogether after independence they nevertheless could become the nucleus of opposition to the government of the day (Meynaud and Bey, 1967). But in any case, whatever their ultimate role, the leaders of trade unions in these countries can learn skills within their organizations which they could not possibly learn elsewhere.

All this means that they constitute a very special elite. In East Africa, for example, where there is a shortage of men for these posts, 'they are confronted by all manner of temptations to exercise power, enter politics, to indulge in what, by their standards, is gracious living' (Allen, 1971). To a considerable degree they are not only socially but physically isolated from the membership. Quite apart from the problem of organizing a system of democratic control amongst the rapidly changing membership which is characteristic of unions of migrant workers, the difficulty of communicating over long distances and the high cost of travel result in conferences of representatives being rarely held. Understandably, in these circumstances, there is a tendency for union leaders to think of themselves as representing the union. They are not, of course, in the position of monarchs or dictators. Indeed, there appears to be 'an incessant and opportunistic struggle between rival contenders for office' (Roberts, 1964) which weakens to a very large extent the personal power of any one of them, although it would be an error to regard this balancing of personalities as being the same thing as the balancing of interests which has been referred to above as the basis of polyarchic government in British trade unions. Many ex-Colonial trade unions are true oligarchies and not polyarchies in this sense.

Moreover, where branch meetings of members are actually held, they are sometimes little more than massive public meetings which by their very size can permit discussion of only very broad and general issues of union policy. Epstein, for example, has described monthly meetings of some eight thousand members of the Roan branch of the African Mine Workers' Trade

Union in Northern Rhodesia (now Zambia) at which rank-and-file members clearly participated. Such meetings can convey a sense of the emotional cohesion of the membership but they inevitably lead to the complaints and problems of aggrieved members being left to the full-time secretary at the branch office to handle. Epstein claims that such a mode of conducting trade union affairs results in it acting as an efficient service organization for the membership (Epstein, 1958) but this is an altogether different conception of trade unionism from that of active member participation in policy making and union government through the election of delegates or representatives whose performance is subject to regular scrutiny by those who elect them.

Nor is it always certain that member interests in general, at least insofar as these are so interpreted by the membership in general, are well served by this system, irrespective of what happens about individual grievances. After independence the Zambian mineworkers' leaders became very much involved in the government's commitment to rapid economic growth. This meant that they thought in national terms of the mining industry in relation to other sections of the developing economy and especially by reference to the government's economic objectives. At the centre, therefore, union leaders were apparently quite willing to succumb to official pressure to contain the demands of the mineworkers *vis-à-vis* other groups in the light of government decided priorities in programmes of industrialization, while the local leaders in the branches were subjected to a continuous barrage from aggrieved and protesting mine employees. This conflict between the frames of reference at different levels of the union may be interpreted as resulting in it being unable 'to perform as a coherent and cohesive organization in support of the government's program' (Bates, 1971), but it might equally be seen as resulting in the inability to satisfy the mineworkers' militant demands for equality in a racially and socially stratified community.

One of the characteristic features which studies of such unions display is the consequence of economic stratification within occupations on the nature of participation in trade unions at the branch level. In the case of the African Mine Workers' Trade Union this takes the form of a disproportionate representation in branch office of employees from the upper levels of the labour force. 'One third of the branch executives occupied training posts for supervisory position, even though supervisors constituted less than one-tenth of the total labour force' (Bates, 1971). Similarly in West Africa in 'almost every branch executive committee' of the Camaroons Development Corporation Workers' Union 'the representatives of a section of unskilled plantation labourers was likely to be an overseer, or another equally senior employee. Branch presidents were often salaried staff in the Junior Service, or even the Intermediate Service of the Corporation; and other branch officers tended to be responsible members of the clerical or executive staff. Conference delegations were composed of the same strata of employee, and, as far as I know, no unskilled labourer has ever been appointed to either a branch executive or the annual conference, despite the fact that some 80% of plantation employees are unskilled labourers' (Warmington, 1960). Of course, this over-representation by higher status employees is not confined to unions in ex-colonial territories. American studies have shown some tendencies for local officers to be elected from higher-paid and more skilled workers with more seniority in both the factory and the union (Strauss and Sayles, 1953b) but not in all unions (Tannenbaum and Kahn). Studies of representation on Workers' Councils in Yugoslavia have shown, similarly, disproportionate composition to the disadvantage of the semi-skilled and unskilled workers with inferior educational attainments (Blumberg, 1968). In this sense there is some support for Michel's contention that educational advantages play some part in the process whereby leaders are selected from the rank-and-file, although, as was pointed out in Chapter VIII (above), as a general rule this does not lead to government by the few—oligarchy—but government by the many, divided in terms of different group interests—polyarchy. In ex-colonial territories, where this polyarchy is very much smaller than in Britain, differentiation is nevertheless not between the top leaders and the rest but between a few activists at various levels of trade union organization and the rest. A typical interpretation of such differentiation in the American context is to argue that just as superior status in the factory is an expression of above-average job performance, so active membership of a trade union is an expression of mental and/or physical superiority (Kyllonen, 1951). The government of trade union branches for plantation and mine, however, suggests that such elite characteristics should not be too readily assumed to be innate. The importance of literacy in the selection of the leadership has already been shown to be significant; and so far as job performance is concerned even purely 'physical' characteristics may have important social determinants—many African workers 'simply do not get enough to eat' (Allen, 1971)—which may also explain in part their apparent unwillingness to offer themselves for office, even to the limited extent which applies elsewhere. The advantage of examining the workings of trade union democracy in ex-colonial territories is that it can serve to prevent too hasty generalization about the selection of the trade union elite in more industrialized communities.

Setting the problem in these terms raises the question of the extent to which there is convergence or divergence in industrializing societies. Are there perhaps structural constraints in industry itself which will mean that once African workers do get enough to eat their trade unions will take on the polyarchic characteristics of the British model? Can we agree with Karl Marx that 'the country that is more developed industrially only shows, to the less developed, the image of its own future'? In Chapter IV—'Collective bargaining under Communism'—it was emphasized that although there are many property and ideological differences between the collectivist industrial relations systems of Russia and Yugoslavia and the more traditionally capitalist system of Britain, the emergence of the shop floor representative as a crucial role-player is common to all, even if the issues about which he negotiates are different. Similarly, in the chapter on business unionism in America it was shown that although the typically 'interest' approach of trade unionists to pressure group politics in that country differed markedly from the welfare 'cause' politics of trade unionists in Britain, the participation of American trade union leaders in the activities of government committees, dealing not only with labour matters but with education, medical services and unemployment benefits, has resulted in them becoming increasingly involved in welfare policy making, both nationally and internationally. The juxtaposition of these two developments—the growing significance of the shop floor representative in the workplace, collective bargaining and the participation of the trade union leader in governmental activities—gives special point to the argument of the previous chapter, that the shop floor representative has also emerged as an important member of the trade union elite. He represents the polyarchic—the non-participating card-carrying member to the official hierarchy, while acting with other shop floor representatives in the collective process whereby leaders are elected and challenged, and the various wishes and interests of the members in different workplaces and localities are balanced one against another.

In countries like Zambia, however, shop stewards have not so much 'emerged' as they have been hastened into existence from above. The African Mine Workers' Trade Union, for example, requires each shop steward to collect twenty-five names of members on a nomination paper before it will confirm him in that office. Thereafter the branch executive repeatedly 'lectures' him on the necessity of being constantly prepared to accept members' grievances. 'To guarantee that shop stewards transmit the grievances through to the branch executive, union leaders require them to report into the union offices on the way home from work' (Bates, 1971). What this means is that the trade union leaders are trying to ensure that workers' grievances are handled by the trade union and are not allowed to build up into some unmanageable force. It is easy to interpret this as a kind of unreasonable perpetuation of the trade union model used by colonial administrators. 'It is the Western-type structure, not collective action itself, which the workers find difficulty in operating' (Allen, 1971). From his experiences in East Africa Allen is convinced that an effective 'indigenous' form of trade unionism could emerge in these ex-colonial territories, but it is not clear whether he has a novel structure in mind or a transformation of the nature of the shop-floor representative's role, once periodic migration ceases to be the characteristic feature of African working-class experience. What he seems to overlook is the extent to which the trade union leaders have deliberately chosen to copy the shop-steward rather than the branch model of union organization, while at the same time endorsing the politician's view of the trade union in these communities as part of the system of control whereby an industrial society may be created. In this sense the kind of shop-floor representative they envisage appearing has more in common with his counterpart in Communist than in Capitalist societies, even where industrial enterprises are still largely financed by foreign investors. The scope of the representative's functions will be much broader than wages and working conditions, and will embrace also education and medical facilities (Davies, 1966). Thus, although the amount of *divergence* which appears open to people to choose in the industrialization process is limited by the nature of those constraints which come from the organization of the enterprise and the large number of union members with which union leaders have to deal, part of the actual *convergence* which occurs comes from the kind of notions about organization which people in less developed areas copy from the more developed. In addition to the unanticipated consequences of industrialization as such, which produce certain features of convergence, there are deliberately willed aspects of convergence which favour some models rather than others. In this respect one of the lessons of this book is that trade unions are not simple responses to the development of an industrial society, but in their own organization and in the impact they make on others they are a creative force responsible for some of the outcomes which are experienced.

Conclusion

CHAPTER XI

Signposts to the Future

The essential feature of a trade union is that it is a continuous association of a life-long class of employees. Thus it was characterized eighty years ago and thus it has been characterized in this account today. Of course it is true that in their original formulation the Webbs wrote of 'wage servants', and thought of the class situation of these servants as intrinsic to capitalism, whereas these ideas have been extended here to include salary earners and workers in enterprises which are not privately but publicly owned. Nevertheless, the class distinction between people who direct industrial operations and those who carry out their instructions, which the Webbs believed to be derived from the distinction between those who owned the means of production and those who were 'divorced' from such ownership, but which has been treated here as a more fundamental division of labour than ownership as such implies, perpetuates the historical separation of the trade union from the guild since the former, unlike the latter, *never* contains amongst its members the 'real directors' of the industry of our time. (S. and B. Webb, 1894.) Trade unions are instruments for collective bargaining with the representatives of directors precisely because there is this class division between them and because their interests in the organization of production conflict. Irrespective of how individuals are selected to become directors, that is to say, their role once selected is to make collective decisions about what is to be produced, how it is to be produced, who is to produce it, and how much the producers will be paid for their efforts. Their willingness to negotiate with trade union representatives over some, or even all, of these decisions should not be misinterpreted to mean that the responsibility to make them lies within the right of their employees to claim. Directors cannot be removed from office by resolution at a trade union meeting. Nor may union representatives negotiate about how directors should make their decisions and what they are to be paid for the work. So long as there is this separation of powers trade unions will continue to be the employees' instrument of collective bargaining, for all that the content of such bargains will vary from country to country, from industry to industry and from firm to firm, according to the operation of the constraints listed on page 55 (above).

The concept of a trade union, in collaboration with other trade unions, as instrument of social change, however, necessarily implies that employees will continue to claim the right to challenge the decisions which directors, as employers, actually make. While their prerogative to make them is not at all in question, bargains may legitimately be made about what is to be produced, how it is to be produced, who is to produce it and how much they are to be paid for it. In this sense the 'new' militancy of today may be seen as motivated by a desire for 'workers' control', that is, by the aim to reduce the range of unrestrained decisions in industry made by employers and their managers. 'When shop stewards operate their own overtime roster, or when they regulate, however informally, the speed of work, or when shop-floor strength and action prevent the carrying out of an arbitrary dismissal, then workers' control is being exercised. The movement to extend the control of workers over arbitrary authority, and over their working environment, is a movement for "workers' control".' (Coates and Topham, 1972.) The notion, touched on in Chapters III and IV (above), that the role of the shop-floor representative in modern industry has been steadily broadened for him to become a linkman between the rank-and-file employee and the managers of his firm, indicates the extent to which such challenges on arbitrariness are now customarily made; for the manager's role is to ensure that the decisions of directors are carried out within the framework of agreements which have already been made between the firm and the union, and his task is made easier if he can convince the workers that any arbitrariness in the situation is beyond his power to remedy. Of course, union representatives may then proceed to negotiate new agreements, but in the meantime a manager may be able, by consulting with them, to keep production going at the agreed price and in the agreed way; and since the shop steward is more likely than the full-time union official to know just how far the workers in his shop will be prepared to co-operate on these terms, it is understandable why shop stewards have come to be so important in recent times.

Clearly, some elements of the situation are beyond the managers' power to remedy because they are beyond the directors' control to decide. The sale of shares by shareholders to an extent that capital becomes difficult for directors to obtain, for example, may cause them to limit expansion, resist wage claims and lay workers off. A decision by a government to channel national resources in one direction rather than another because of the priority given, say, to defence may similarly force the directors of a nationally owned industry to curtail production, shut down plant and in other ways retrench. Trade unionists will see in these reactions a threat to the level of living of employees in these and related firms and industries, which collective bargaining with directors and their representatives can do little to remove. Hence arises the political response of the trade unions, inspired perhaps by a belief in the superior efficiency of public as opposed to private enterprise or in the capacity of parliament to determine a government's apportioning of state expenditure. Purely in terms of member interests trade unions become pressure groups, although as Chapter VII indicated, even the most reluctant of them find themselves increasingly involved in programmes of social reform as opposed to member defence merely. Contemporary governments involve themselves more and more in decisions which directly influence the working of the economy, and to the degree that they do this, trade union leaders work for workers' control by challenging the arbitrariness of the decisions which are made. Yet so long as they remain trade unionists and do not set up their unions as political parties, ready to take over the government of the country, they are limiting their challenge to the content of those decisions and not extending it to abrogate the politician's rights to make them by legislations, in the broadest sense of that term. Just as the amount of workers' control envisaged for the enterprise stops short of abolishing directors altogether, so the control for the economy stops short of abolishing the political machine; and as the trade unions move into the twenty-first century these two limitations on the horizon of their objectives indicate the extent to which trade unionism as a social philosophy accepts the class system which the passing of classical capitalism has bequeathed to the industrial employee. For all that its emphasis is collectivist it does not envisage a classless, collectivist society as a likelihood, or even a possibility.

Within their own organizations, of course, trade unionists do not accept these limitations. Although the directors of enterprises cannot be removed from office by resolution at any trade union meeting, trade union leaders can, through a well-defined procedure. The Amalgamated Society of Woodworkers, for example, can dismiss its general secretary by a vote of members; the Electrical Trades Union has a similar provision in its rules; and nearly every British trade union rule-book provides that the Executive Council of the union can dismiss such officials for fraud, misdemeanour or incompetence, even if such contingencies rarely occur (Roberts, 1956). Similarly, although trade union representatives cannot negotiate about how directors of enterprises may make decisions which affect the livelihood of their members, or what they are to be paid for so doing, they can negotiate with their own employees, the full-time officials on precisely these issues (Clegg, Killick and Adams, 1961). Members' control *within* trade unions means the operation of a democratic ideology in which each member has no more than one vote and each member is expected to take an equal share of responsibility for making decisions.

The persistence of such an ideology in spite of the difficulties of large-scale organization and the unwillingness to extend the ideology practically into a demand for the control of the industrial enterprise may be explained in terms of the fact that trade unions are, in fact, employee-class organizations. Irrespective of differences in their individual skills and achievements and in the wages or salaries they receive, all workers are in the same class position *vis-à-vis* their employers. Combination amongst themselves to bargain collectively with employers implies that in *this* relationship the similarity between them as employees outweighs the differences between them as individuals; and equality between them in the organizations which represent their class interests is the simplest form by which to ensure that each individual point of view may be expressed. Inevitably, of course, as the last part of this book has demonstrated, once these class organizations become large the differences between groups of them emerge as *interests other than class interests* which divide them. This is why trade unions are polyarchies rather than simple democracies. The Webbs' conception of the trade union as an association of a life-long class of employees needs to be supplemented at this point by the more historically general concept of the division of interests which accompanies the division of labour. Not only are there separate unions for different 'trades', or in the Communist case for different industries, but within each union different kinds of employment lead to group alignments, divisive within the same class position. For all that trade unions substitute collective decision-making for economic individualism, there is no indication that in the foreseeable future their efforts to change the economic system are going to result in a form of collectivism without class or interest conflicts to succeed the capitalist system which initially gave rise to trade unionism.

Nor does it follow that the emphasis on the trade union as a class organization will result in interests other than class interests becoming necessarily defined solely in terms of the division of labour. As was pointed out in the American context, the desire on the part of trade unionists to reduce competition between workers by limiting the access of whole categories of people to certain jobs has sometimes taken the form of discrimination against minorities, especially negroes (page 78 above). It has also taken the form in America and elsewhere of discrimination against women. Skilled workers in Britain, in particular, maintained an attitude of 'woman's place is in the home' for most of the nineteenth century (Trades Union Congress, 1955). Of course, such discrimination has often been 'justified' on the ground that the minority member's capacity for the work in question has been 'naturally' inferior, although the evidence on which to base such an inference has usually been lacking and likely to remain so while effective discrimination prevented such individuals from demonstrating their capacity. The point of substance in discrimination is that it could be easily applied wherever a minority group was easily recognizable, because of some biological characteristic such as sex or skin colour, or because of some marked cultural trait which showed itself in dress, toilet or feeding behaviours quite distinct from those of the majority group. Where, in the future, some group of English trade unionists believe their livelihood to be threatened because of an influx to their region of employment by some such readily observable minority group, such as Indians, Pakistanis or West Indians, the possibility of minority discrimination on the part of the dominant group is likely. The class organization of the trade union movement does not mean that the rank-and-file workers of the world will inevitably unite.

If these are the first major conclusions which a sociologist must draw from his analysis of the nature and significance of trade unionism in the contemporary world, the second is that the emergence of the shop-floor representative as a crucial figure in workplace organization is a consequence of the kind of collectivism which has actually occurred with the decline of individualism. The chief feature of this system is that the modern industrial enterprise is a large-scale organization in which the directors, who make decisions influencing the destinies of thousands of people, are separated by many levels of intermediaries from the men who actually do the work. Such multi-level organizations are characteristic not only of industry but of politics, as well as of trade unionism itself, as the diagrams on pages 21 and 80 (above) indicate. Yet the issues with which trade unions are concerned, and which justify their continued existence, are the 'business' of their rank-and-file members, however much this business may sometimes be obscured by questions of 'the national interest' or concern for 'the future of the labour movement' (Allen, 1966). The matching of three hierarchies, level by level, in terms of representatives of the trade union as negotiator with representatives of employers, on the one hand, and as lobbyist with representatives of the legislature, on the other, is a device within such a system of hierarchical organization for ensuring that the worker's interests as employee and as citizen are taken into account.

In terms of authority, however, the line of command runs from top to bottom in both the employing and the legislating systems, and although it would be a mistake to argue that it runs from bottom to top in the trade union, it is nevertheless clear that the trade union organization differs from the other two in this respect of authority. Because of the trade union leader's responsibility to the rank-and-file member, he is unable to issue instructions which are analogous to those issued by directors to the hierarchies under their command of employment and by legislators to those under their command of enactment. The notion that trade unions are oligarchies, to be sure, turns on the assumption that as a matter of fact this is precisely what trade union leaders do; but the rejection of this notion, as in Chapter V, in favour of trade unions as polyarchies, stresses the extent to which the class-conflict basis of trade unionism perpetuates within it an 'iron law' of democracy which is transmuted from primitive to representative democracy by the exigencies of organizational imperatives. This means that the ordinary rank-and-file member can participate satisfactorily only when he is representative of a number of his fellows, and this representation seems to achieve its most viable form in large-scale enterprise and large-scale trade unionism at the shop-floor, rather than the branch, level. If industrial organizations continue to grow larger, either through amalgamation or nationalization, and if governments continue to enact more and more legislation which makes its impact directly on the lives of their citizens, trade unions will continue to become even more necessary as effective organizations of representative democracy. In the process the English shop steward, and his counterpart in other societies, will become an even more important figure in the trade union world.

This book has attempted to provide a sociological framework for understanding the nature of this world at the present time. Inevitably, it has been obliged to ignore certain issues which might well have been thought important. For example, one of the enduring British concerns at the moment is inflation, and although a sociologist might claim exemption from tackling a problem more properly that of the economist, it cannot be denied that an essential feature of contemporary industrial negotiation and of government legislation centres upon the determination to curb what are recognized as the unsatisfactory consequences of a steady devaluation of the currency. Nevertheless, although it is clear that such phenomena as inflation are important *constraints* on what goes on in an industrial relations system or a lobbying system and must therefore be considered in the examination of *any specific* case of trade union activity, they may be correctly seen as *external* to these systems, in the sense of Chapter II (above), and may legitimately be omitted in a book of this size. It should be noticed, however, that to the degree that a government attempts to restrict wage and salary demands by employees as contrary to the public interest, to this degree will trade unionists interpret this definition of public interest as the class interest of their members' employers in disguise. The separate diagrams on pages 21 and 80 (above) should, that is to say, not be read as two quite distinct systems. Insofar as the trade unions are involved in both, the activities of negotiators *and* lobbyists are directed towards the same general ends—the improvement of the position in society of the trade union member—and the reactions of employers and administrators interpreted in the same general terms. Thus, although throughout this book attention has been concentrated on the characteristic features of the *internal* organizations of trade unions as instruments of collective bargaining, social change and democratic participation, the more complete analysis of industrial relations systems and movements of constructive social change as such requires more detailed sociological investigation than has been possible here.

In passing, it should also be emphasized that the analysis has also stopped short at the boundaries of the nation state. Yet, as was mentioned on page 69, every summer a number of the T.U.C. General Council members spend five weeks at the International Labour Conference, an organization which draws together representatives of governments, employers and trade unions from one hundred and twenty-five countries of the world. At first sight, therefore, it might seem that the structure of relationships, simplified in the diagrams, really indicates a worldwide, rather than a nation-bound phenomenon. The I.L.O., however, does not possess the powers which such a conclusion would imply. For all that it can try to persuade the representatives from one nation to adopt what it recommends as better standards, as in the case of the negotiation machinery of the British Merchant Navy (Stewart, 1969), or more generally, adopt minimum standards for contracts of employment, permit workers to join trade unions, and encourage collective bargaining for the settlement of disputes (Alcock, 1971), the function of the

I.L.O. is to assist other people, not to decide for them (Johnston, 1970). Collective bargaining and legislation *are* nation-bound, although participation in such international gatherings forms part of the environment which constrains certain aspects of what is done in the various national systems in which trade unions are involved. Such participation by trade union leaders, certainly, takes them into a world of experience, largely beyond the grasp of the imaginations of rank-and-file members, and in this sense the world outlook of a modern trade union may be seen as a further complication in the communication system which links the top and the bottom of the trade union movement.

Much the same kind of consideration also applies to the development in recent times of the multi-national firm and its corollary; the multi-national trade union, formed by workers in the chemical, food and drink, metal, and electrical industries (Levinson, 1972). As yet, these international organizations and collective bargaining at an international level have not proceeded so far that national systems of collective bargaining, pressure group politics and internal trade union democracy have been much influenced by them. Multi-national political devices for economic purposes, such as the Common Market, however, may eventually produce co-ordinated trade union activity at a multi-national level, whence the kind of analysis in this book will have to be extended to this level. Trade union democracy, for example, will perforce need to be examined in the polyarchic form where trade unionists from one nation will pursue interests which are not shared by those from another. But all this lies in the future.

Concentration at the national level has, of course, made possible the kind of comparisons set out in this book, between the different kinds of collective bargaining which occur under a system of largely private ownership of industrial property (Britain) as compared with public ownership (Communist Societies), between different kinds of pressure-group politics when the dominant trade-union ideology is anti-capitalist (Britain) and anti-individualist (America), between different kinds of union organization when literacy is high and the industrial system relatively old (Britain) and when literacy is low and industrialism novel (Africa). There is no assumption about convergence here. All these systems are changing to some degree, but there is no evidence that they must *necessarily* become the same, although there is evidence that some copying occurs, just as there is evidence of a deliberate rejection of another nation's model. What are the possibilities that Russian trade unionists will set out to incorporate some feature of the American system into their own? Or the American some feature of the Russian?

Inevitably, however, the concentration in these comparisons on Britain has meant that the characteristics of Communist trade unionism which have been emphasized are those of collective bargaining, not of pressure group politics or trade union democracy, and it should not be assumed that there are no differences worthy of consideration, between the British and, say, the Russian trade union movements in these respects. The present book has been written to indicate how a sociological analysis may be conducted. It does not constitute a substantive account of every aspect of trade unionism in those other countries. They have, indeed, been chosen deliberately to bring out the essential features of the British case, not as cases in their own right; and the British case indicates that the journey to the twenty-first century is being made by the British trade union movement in its idiosyncratic way, for all that certain aspects of its experience—the importance of the shop-floor representative as the link-man with industry, and the trade union leader as the link-man with government, for example—set constraints on how idiosyncratic it may be. Sociology, it must be emphasized, deals with probabilities, not with certainties, but it has predictive power because human behaviour occurs by reference to constraints which may be identified and is not entirely capricious or random.

Bibliography

A complete bibliography of trade unionism, even for the limited number of countries covered here, would be enormous. In a book of this size, therefore, some selection is inevitable. Hence the works which are listed below are only those which have been referred to in the text. Not all of them are directly concerned with collective bargaining, pressure group union politics, trade union democracy, or a combination of these topics. They have been chosen nevertheless because of their relevance to the arguments presented and should be consulted primarily in these terms. Given the emphasis of the book, most of the references are to sources of information about British trade unionism. However, to assist the reader to find the references to trade unionism in the other countries more rapidly a listing of these precedes the full list. No attempt is made to cover these countries in detail. The interested reader is, accordingly, referred to the relevant sections of ALLEN, Victor L. (1968) *International Bibliography of Trade Unionism*. London: Merlin Press, which *inter alia* includes 51 items of earlier bibliographies, anthologies, research guides and source material. Readers especially interested in the history of British trade unionism will find 61 references in Allen. They might also like to consult FROW, Ruth and Edmund, and KATANKA, M. (1969) *The History of British Trade Unionism: a Select Bibliography*. London: Historical Association Pamphlet H.76; and the Select Bibliography in MUSSON, Albert E. (1972) *British Trade Unions, 1800-1875*. London: Macmillan: 68-76.

Works in the bibliography which refer to specified countries

COMMUNIST SOCIETIES

Blumberg (1968); Brown (1966); Deutscher (1950); Dunlop (1958); International Labour Office (1960b, 1963); Kolaja (1960, 1965), McAuley (1969); Nove (1965); Riddell (1968); Sturmthall (1964); Supek (1970); Webb (1935).

AMERICAN TRADE UNIONS

Barbash (1963, 1972); Bell (1958); Dean (1954a, 1954b); Derber and Young (1957); Dunlop (1958); Edelstein *et al.* (1970); International Labour Office

(1960a); Karson (1958); Kyllonen (1951); Leiserson (1959); Lipset *et al.* (1956); Marshall (1965); Mills (1948); Morris (1958); Purcell (1953); Raphael (1965); Sayles and Strauss (1953); Strauss and Sayles (1953a, 1953b); Taft (1957, 1959); Tagliacozzo and Seidman (1956); Tannenbaum and Kahn (1958); Ulman (1961); Walton and McKersie (1965); Wilensky (1956).

AFRICAN TRADE UNIONISM

Allen (1971); Bates (1971); Davies (1966); Epstein (1958); Meynaud and Bey (1967); Millen (1963); Roberts (1964); Scott (1966); Warmington (1960).

REFERENCES

ALCOCK, ANTHONY (1971). *History of the International Labour Organization.* London: Macmillan.

ALLEN, VICTOR L. (1957). *Trade Union Leadership: based on a study of Arthur Deakin.* London: Longmans Green. Part I deals with the history of the leadership of the Transport and General Workers' Union.

ALLEN, VICTOR L. (1960). *Trade Unions and the Government.* London: Longmans Green. Deals with trade unions as pressure groups etc. and provides a detailed history of trade unions and the Labour Governments, 1924-1951.

ALLEN, VICTOR L. (1966). *Militant Trade Unionism.* London: Merlin Press. Subtitled: 'a re-analysis of industrial action in an inflationary situation', this study discusses militancy in the context of crises from 1947 to 1964 and fallacies about strikes and wages.

ALLEN, VICTOR L. (1971). *The Sociology of Industrial Relations.* London: Longman. A collection of essays on various topics. Part III deals with the history of the T.U.C. and Part IV with trade unionism in the developing economies of Africa.

ANDERSON, PERRY (1967). 'The Limits and Possibilities of Trade Union Action' in BLACKBURN and COCKBURN (1967). An examination of the role of trade unions in the socialist movement and the future tasks of British trade unions in a capitalist economy.

BAIN, GEORGE S. (1967). 'Trade Union Growth and Recognition'. *Research Papers 6: Royal Commission on Trade Unions and Employers' Associations.* London: H.M.S.O. A study of white-collar unions in private industry from 1917 to the present day.

BAIN, GEORGE S. (1970). *The Growth of White-Collar Unionism.* Oxford: Clarendon Press. A study of the factors promoting and hindering the growth of trade unions amongst white-collar workers, especially from 1948 to 1964.

BANKS, JOSEPH A. (1970). *Marxist Sociology in Action: a Sociological Critique of the Marxist Approach to Industrial Relations.* London: Faber and Faber. An attempt to test the Marxist account of trade unionism empirically, largely by reference to the British steel industry since the industrial revolution.

BANKS, JOSEPH A. (1972). *The Sociology of Social Movements.* London: Macmillan. An attempt to apply an action frame of reference to constructive social movements, with some reference to trade unions.

BARBASH, JACK (1963). 'The Government and Politics of the AFL-CIO' in SOMERS, GERALD G. ed.: *Labor, Management and Social Policy.* Madison: University of Wisconsin Press.

BARBASH, JACK (1972). *Trade Unions and National Economic Policy.* Baltimore:

The John Hopkins Press. Chapter 6 deals with British trade union involvement in national economic policy and Chapter 9 with the implications of Western European experience for the United States.

BARRY, E. ELDON (1965). *Nationalisation in British Politics: the Historical Background.* Cape: London. Covers the period 1851-1951 in chronological terms.

BATES, ROBERT H. (1971). *Unions, Parties, and Political Development.* New Haven: Yale University Press. Subtitled 'a study of mineworkers in Zambia', it includes an analysis of disputes between 1950 and 1968.

BEAN, RONALD (1965). 'Militancy, Policy Formation and Membership Opposition in the Electrical Trades Union, 1945-61.' *The Political Quarterly,* 36: 181-190. An analysis of policy conference resolutions.

BEER, MAX (1957). *The General History of Socialism and Social Struggles,* 1. New York: Russell and Russell. Covers the period from antiquity to the end of the Middle Ages.

BELL, DANIEL (1958). 'The Capitalism of the Proletariat', *Encounter,* February 1958, reprinted in his *The End of Ideology* (New York: Collier Books, 1961). An examination of American trade unions as aggressive bargaining organizations.

BLACKBURN, ROBERT M. (1967). *Union Character and Social Class: a Study of White-Collar Unionism.* London: Batsford. A study of trade unionism in banking, including a survey of bank clerks.

BLACKBURN, R. M. and PRANDY, K. (1965). 'White-Collar Unionization: a Conceptual Framework'. *The British Journal of Sociology,* 16: 111-122.

BLACKBURN, ROBIN and COCKBURN, ALEXANDER, eds. (1967). *The Incompatibles: Trade Union Militancy and the Consensus.* Harmondsworth: Penguin Books. A collection of articles on contemporary British trade union issues from a *New Left Review* angle.

BLAIN, A. N. J. and GENNARD, JOHN (1970). 'Industrial Relations Theory—A Critical Review'. *British Journal of Industrial Relations,* 8. An examination of the work of Dunlop, Flanders and Clegg, and conflict theorists.

BLUMBERG, PAUL (1968). *Industrial Democracy.* London: Constable. Subtitled 'the sociology of participation', this study has an examination of Hugh Clegg's notions of industrial democracy (Chapter 7) and two chapters on workers' management in Jugoslavia (Chapters 8 and 9).

BRENTANO, LUJO (1870). *On the History and Development of Gilds and the Origin of Trade-Unions.* London: Truebner.

BROWN, EMILY C. (1966). *Soviet Trade Unions and Labor Relations.* Cambridge, Massachusetts: Harvard University Press. A study based on Soviet records and interviews with Soviet industrial and trade union leaders, etc., in 1955, 1959 and 1962.

BURNHAM, JAMES (1942). *The Managerial Revolution.* London: Putnam. A theory that managers in Russia, Germany and the United States were moving towards social dominance in the 1930's by shifting the locus of political sovereignty in their economic favour.

BUTLER, DAVID and FREEMAN, JENNIE (1969). *British Political Facts 1900-1968,* 3rd edition. London: Macmillan. A compendium of statistics, Chapter 2 has details on sponsored M.P.'s and Chapter 10 on trade unions.

BUTLER, DAVID and STOKES, DONALD (1969). *Political Change in Britain.* London: Macmillan. Chapter 7 deals with trade union membership and allegiance with the Labour Party.

CLEGG, HUGH A. (1951). *Industrial Democracy and Nationalization.* Oxford: Blackwell. Considers the meaning of the term, 'industrial democracy', historically and in connection with decentralization and other problems of British nationalized industries.

CLEGG, HUGH (1964). *General Union in a Changing Society.* Oxford: Blackwell. A short history of the National Union of General and Municipal Workers, 1889-1964.

CLEGG, HUGH A., KILLICK, A. J., and ADAMS, R. (1962). *Trade Union Officers.* Oxford: Blackwell. A study of union records and questionnaire surveys of full-time union officers, branch secretaries and shop stewards in British trade unions.

CLEGG, HUGH *et al.* (1964). *A History of British Trade Unions since 1889,* 1 (1889-1910). Oxford: Clarendon Press.

COATES, KEN, ed. (1968). *Can the Workers Run Industry?* London: Sphere Books. A series of essays by trade unionists and others on who controls the British economy and on conditions in specific industries.

COATES, KEN and TOPHAM, A. (1972). *The New Unionism : the Case for Workers' Control.* London: Owen.

COLE, GEORGE D. H. (1944). *A Century of Co-operation.* Manchester: Co-operative Union. Chapter 20 deals with co-operative employment and trade unions in the British co-operative movement.

COLE, GEORGE D. H. (1953). *Attempts at General Union: a Study in British Trade Union History, 1818-1834.* London: Macmillan.

COMMISSION ON INDUSTRIAL RELATIONS (1971). 'Facilities Afforded to Shop Stewards'. [Report No. 17.] London: H.M.S.O., Cmnd. 4668. A policy statement on the arrangements which should be made to enable workplace representations to carry out their functions effectively.

DAVIES, IOAN (1966). *African Trade Unions.* Harmondsworth: Penguin Books. An account of the changing economic structure of African societies from colonial times and the role of trade unions in economic development since independence.

DEAN, L. R. (1954a). 'Social integration, attitudes, and union activity'. *Industrial and Labor Relations Review,* 8 (1954): 48-58.

DEAN, L. R. (1954b). 'Union Activity and Dual Loyalty'. *Industrial and Labor Relations Review,* 7: 526-536.

DEPARTMENT OF EMPLOYMENT (1971). 'The Reform of Collective Bargaining at Plant and Company Level'. *Manpower Papers No. 5.* London: H.M.S.O. A set of case studies by the Research and Planning Division of the Department, conducted in eleven firms in 1969 and 1970.

DERBER, MILTON and YOUNG, E., eds. (1957). *Labor and the New Deal.* University of Wisconsin Press.

DEUTSCHER, ISAAC (1950). *Soviet Trade Unions.* London: Royal Institute of International Affairs. An analysis of the changing role of trade unions in the planned economy of the U.S.S.R.

DONOVAN (1968). *Royal Commission on Trade Unions and Employers' Associations 1965-1968. Chairman: the Rt. Hon. Lord Donovan.* London: H.M.S.O., Cmnd. 3623.

DONOVAN SECRETARIAT (1967). '1. Productivity Bargaining. 2. Restrictive Labour Practices'. *Research Papers 4, Royal Commission on Trade Unions and Employers' Associations.* London. H.M.S.O. A summary of information and views of many industrialists on productivity bargaining.

DUNLOP, JOHN T. (1958). *Industrial Relations Systems.* New York: Holt.

EDELSTEIN, J. D. (1964-5). 'Democracy in a National Union: the British A.E.U.'. *Industrial Relations,* 4: 105-125. An analysis of the elections of General Secretaries and Presidents, 1875-1964.

EDELSTEIN, J. D. (1968). 'Countervailing Powers and the Political Process in the

British Mineworkers' Union'. *International Journal of Comparative Sociology*, 9: 255-288. An analysis of the election of General Secretaries and Presidents, 1918-1960.

EDELSTEIN, J. D. *et al.* (1970). 'The Pattern of Opposition in British and American Unions'. *Sociology*, 4: 145-163. A survey of electoral results in 31 British and 51 American manual workers' unions.

EPSTEIN, ARNOLD L. (1958). *Politics in an Urban African Community*. Manchester University Press. An anthropological study of Luanshya, Northern Rhodesia, carried out from August 1953 to June 1954 in a coppermine town.

FERRIS, PAUL (1972). *The New Militants: Crisis in the Trade Unions*. Harmondsworth: Penguin Books. A journalist's view of contemporary trade unionism in British society.

FINER, SAMUEL E. (1958). *Anonymous Empire: a Study of the Lobby in Great Britain*. London: Pall Mall Press. A political scientist's examination of pressure group politics, including pressures by trade union leaders and businessmen on Whitehall and Westminster.

FLANDERS, ALLEN (1964). *The Fawley Productivity Agreements*. London: Faber and Faber. A study of the negotiations between the managers of the Esso oil refinery at Fawley and the trade unions on the agreement of 1960 and subsequently.

FLANDERS, ALLEN (1968). 'Bargaining Theory: the Classical Model Reconsidered' in ROBERTS, BEN C.

FOX, ALAN (1966). 'Industrial Sociology and Industrial Relations'. *Research Papers 3, Royal Commission on Trade Unions and Employers' Associations*. London: H.M.S.O. Subtitled 'an assessment of the contribution which industrial sociology can make towards understanding and resolving some of the problems now being considered by the Royal Commission', the emphasis is laid on industrial organizations as coalitions of interests between managers and workers, represented by trade unions.

FOX, ALAN (1971). *A Sociology of Work in Industry*. Collier-Macmillan: London. Chapter 4 deals with 'employee collectivities', power concentrations, institutionalized in conflict with management.

GOLDTHORPE, JOHN H. *et al.* (1968). *The Affluent Worker: Political Attitudes and Behaviour*. Cambridge University Press. Vol. 2 of the 'Affluent Worker' study of manual and clerical workers in Luton, England, 1962-64.

GOODMAN, JOHN F. B. and WHITTINGHAM, T. G. (1969). *Shop Stewards in British Industry*. London: McGraw-Hill. A historical account supplemented by a postal questionnaire enquiry amongst shop stewards in 1964-7 and diaries of the activities of 19 stewards over a two-month period.

HARRISON, MARTIN (1960). *Trade Unions and the Labour Party since 1945*. London: Allen and Unwin.

HOBHOUSE, LEONARD T. (1906). *The Labour Movement*, 2nd edition. London: Allen and Unwin. Chapter 2 deals with trade unionism and the control of production from a liberal journalist's point of view.

HOWELL, GEORGE (1878). *The Conflicts of Capital and Labour*. London: Chatto and Windus. A history of trade unionism and the guilds.

HOWELL, GEORGE (1891). *Trade Unionism: New and Old*. London: Methuen. Mainly concerned with the new unionism of the period, preceded by a historical sketch of guilds and trade unions.

HYMAN, RICHARD (1972). *Strikes*. London: Collins. A sociological analysis of industrial conflict and strikes in the British industrial relations system.

IN PLACE OF STRIFE (1969). *A Policy for Industrial Relations, presented to Parliament by the First Secretary of State and Secretary of State for Em-*

ployment and Productivity. London: H.M.S.O., Cmnd. 3888. A Labour Minister's policy statement, proposing an Industrial Relations Act, following the Donovan Report.

INTERNATIONAL LABOUR OFFICE (1960a). *The Trade Union Situation in the United States*. Geneva: I.L.O. Report from an I.L.O. mission to the United States, March to June, 1959.

INTERNATIONAL LABOUR OFFICE (1960b). *The Trade Union Situation in the U.S.S.R.* Geneva: I.L.O. Report of an I.L.O. mission to the Soviet Union, August to October, 1959.

INTERNATIONAL LABOUR OFFICE (1963). *Workers' Management in Yugoslavia*. Geneva: I.L.O.

JEWELL, MALCOLM E. and PATTERSON, SAMUEL C. (1966). *The Legislative Process in the United States*. New York: Random House.

JOHNSTON, GEORGE A. (1970). *The International Labour Organization*. London: Europa Publications. An historical and contemporary analysis of policies, problems and programmes.

KARSON, MARC (1958). *American Labor Unions and Politics 1900-1918*. Carbondate: Southern Illinois University Press.

KOLAJA, JIRI (1960). *A Polish Factory: A Case Study of Workers' Participation in Decision Making*. University of Kentucky Press. A study of a workers' council in a Lodz textile factory.

KOLAJA, JIRI (1965). *Workers' Councils: the Yugoslav Experience*. Tavistock Publications: London. A study of two factories in Belgrade.

KYLLONEN, T. E. (1951). 'Social Characteristics of Active Unionists'. *The American Journal of Sociology*, 56: 528-533. A report on interviews with 183 employers in a small mid-Missouri factory.

LANE, ANTHONY and ROBERTS, KENNETH (1971). *Strike at Pilkingtons*. London: Collins. A sociological survey of a strike at the Pilkington Brothers' factory in St. Helens, England, April to March, 1970.

LEISERSON, WILLIAM M. (1959). *American Trade Union Democracy*. New York: Columbia University Press. A historical and documentary analysis.

LEVINSON, CHARLES (1972). *International Trades Unionism*. London: Allen and Unwin. A study of the trade union response to the multinational corporation in a number of industries.

LIPSET, SEYMOUR M. *et al.* (1956). *Union Democracy*. Glencoe, Illinois: The Free Press. A sociological survey of the history and current practices and attitudes in the American International Typographical Union, 1951-52.

LIPSON, EPHRAIM (1947). *The Economic History of England*, 1: 'The Middle Ages', 9th edition. London: Adam and Charles Black. Chapter 8 deals with the craft guilds.

LOZOVSKY, ALEKSANDER (1935). *Marx and the Trade Unions*. London: Laurence. A description of the position taken by Marx and Engels on the role of trade unions in the revolutionary overthrow of the capitalist class system.

MARGERISON, CHARLES J. (1969). 'What do we mean by industrial relations? A behavioural science approach'. *British Journal of Industrial Relations*, 7.

MARSH, ARTHUR I. and MCCARTHY, W. E. J. (1968). 'Disputes Procedures in Britain'. *Research Papers 2 (Part 2), Royal Commission on Trade Unions and Employers' Associations*. London: H.M.S.O. An examination of the operation of procedural agreements in engineering, paper-making, chemical, building and coalmining industries.

MARSHALL, RAY (1965). *The Negro and Organized Labor*. New York: Wiley. A historical and general survey of American unionism.

MCAULEY, MARY (1969). *Labour Disputes in Soviet Russia 1957-1965*. Oxford:

Clarendon Press. An examination of disputes within the enterprise and in the courts.

MCCARTHY, WILLIAM E. J. (1964). *The Closed Shop in Britain*. Oxford: Blackwell. A description of the functions of the closed shop in a number of British trade unions and of its legal and ideological justification.

MCCARTHY, WILLIAM E. J. (1967). 'The Role of Shop Stewards in British Industrial Relations'. *Research Papers 1, Royal Commission on Trade Union and Employers' Associations*. London: H.M.S.O. A survey of the literature, supplemented by unpublished work carried out by McCarthy and E. Coker with trade unions.

MCCARTHY, WILLIAM E. J. and PARKER, S. R. (1968). 'Shop Stewards and Workshop Relations'. *Research Papers 10, Royal Commission on Trade Unions and Employers' Associations*. London: H.M.S.O. A report on a series of surveys carried out by the Government Social Survey amongst a sample of trade union officers and shop stewards in six large unions.

MEYNAUD, JEAN and BEY, A. S. (1967). *Trade Unionism in Africa*. London: Methuen. An historical account, with special reference to nationalist politics, colonial independence, and African trade unionism in the international trade union movement.

MILLEN, BRUCE H. (1963). *The Political Role of Labor in Developing Countries*. Washington: Brookings Institution. A general survey of developments in Asia and Africa.

MILLS, CHARLES W. (1948). *The New Men of Power: America's Labor Leaders*. New York: Harcourt, Bruce.

MINISTRY OF LABOUR (1960). *Industrial Relations Handbook*. London: H.M.S.O. An official description of collective bargaining and joint negotiation machinery etc. between organizations of employers and trade unions in Great Britain.

MORRIS, JAMES O. (1958). *Conflict within the A.F. of L.* Cornell University Press. Primarily concerned with the rise of the C.I.O. within the A.F. of L. and the eventual split.

NOVE, ALEC (1965). *The Soviet Economy*, 2nd edition (revised). London: Allen and Unwin.

PARSONS, TALCOTT and SMELSER, NEIL J. (1956). *Economy and Society: A Study in the Integration of Economic and Social Theory*. London: Routledge and Kegan Paul. Presents a functionalist analysis of social systems and the place of the economy within them, with the role of trade unions seen as intermediary between the household and the firm.

PELLING, HENRY (1965). *The Origins of the Labour Party 1880-1900*, 2nd edition. Oxford: Clarendon Press. Chapter 5 deals with the impact of the unskilled workers' unions and Chapter 10 with the conversion of trade unions to support the new Party.

POTTER, BEATRICE (1891). *The Co-operative Movement in Great Britain*. London: Allen and Unwin. Chapter 7 deals with collective bargaining.

PRIBIĆEVIĆ, BRANKO (1954). *The Shop Stewards' Movement and Workers' Control 1910-1922*. Oxford: Blackwell. A general historical study with special reference to the engineering workers, particularly during the First World War.

PURCELL, THEODORE V. (1953). *The Worker Speaks his Mind on Company and Union*. Cambridge, Massachusetts: Harvard University Press.

RAPHAEL, E. E. (1965). 'Power Structure and Membership Dispersal in Unions.' *American Journal of Sociology*, 71: 271-283. The documents of a weighted sample of 65 local unions on Chicago and Cash County, Illinois, were studied for information on the size of the membership and their geographical location, etc.

RIDDELL, DAVID S. (1968). 'Social self-government: the background of theory and practice in Yugoslav socialism'. *The British Journal of Sociology*, 19: 47-75.

ROBERTS, BENJAMIN C. (1956). *Trade Union Government and Administration in Great Britain*. London: Bell and Sons.

ROBERTS, BENJAMIN C. (1958). *The Trades Union Congress 1868-1921*. London: Allen and Unwin.

ROBERTS, BENJAMIN C. (1964). *Labour in the Tropical Territories of the Commonwealth*. London: Bell and Sons. Deals with the development of trade unions, labour policy, labour law and industrial relations, especially since 1938.

ROBERTS, BENJAMIN C., ed. (1968). *Industrial Relations: Contemporary Issues*. London: Macmillan. Papers of the First World Congress of the International Industrial Relations Association, 1967; Part I deals with bargaining and conflict theories.

ROBERTS, B. C. and GENNARD, J. (1970). 'Trends in Plant and Company Bargaining' in ROBERTSON and HUNTER, eds. (1970), 31-50.

ROBERTS, BRYN (1961). *The Price of T.U.C. Leadership*. London: Allen and Unwin. An analysis of Congresses from 1952-1959 in terms of the powers of major unions.

ROBERTSON, DONALD J. and HUNTER, L. C., eds. (1970). *Labour Market Issues of the 1970s*. Edinburgh: Oliver and Boyd.

ROLPH, CECIL (1962). *All Those in Favour?* London: Deutsch. An account of the High Court action against the officers of the Electrical Trades Union for ballot-rigging, 1961.

SAYLES, LEONARD R. and STRAUSS, G. (1953). *The Local Union*. New York: Harper. A report on research conducted by unsystematic interviewing in 20 local unions in 4 north-eastern American communities.

SCOTT, ROGER (1966). *The Development of Trade Unions in Uganda 1966*. Nairobi: East African Publishing House.

SMELSER, NEIL J. (1959). *Social Change in the Industrial Revolution*. London: Routledge and Kegan Paul. Chapter 12 deals with the evolution of trade unions, 1770 to 1840, in the Lancashire Cotton industry.

STEWART, MARGARET (1969). *Britain and the I.L.O.: The Story of Fifty Years*. London: H.M.S.O.

STRAUSS, G. and SAYLES, S. R. (1953a). 'The Local union meeting'. *Industrial and Labor Relations Review*, 6 (1953): 206-219.

STRAUSS, G. and SAYLES, L. R. (1953b). 'Occupation and the Selection of Local Union Officers'. *The American Journal of Sociology*, 58: 585-591. A survey based on interviews in 20 local unions.

STURMATHAL, ADOLF (1964). *Workers' Councils: A Study of Workplace Organization on both sides of the Iron Curtain*. Cambridge, Massachusetts: Harvard University Press. Chapter 4 deals with Yugoslavia and Chapter 5 with Poland.

SUPEK, RUDI (1970). 'Problems and Perspectives of Workers' Self-management in Yugoslavia' in M. J. BROEKMEYER, ed. *Yugoslav Workers' Self-management*. Dordrecht: Reidel.

TAFT, PHILIP (1957). *The A.F. of L. in the Time of Gompers*. New York: Harper. Covers the period of American trade union history from the early nineteenth century to the end of the First World War.

TAFT, PHILIP (1959). *The A.F. of L. from the Death of Gompers to the Merger*.

New York: Harper. Covers the period from the end of the First World War until the A.F. of L. and C.I.O. merger in 1955.

TAGLIACOZZO, E. L. and SEIDMAN, J. (1956). 'A typology of rank-and-file union members'. *American Journal of Sociology*, 61 (1956), 546-558. Interviews with samples of members in three American local unions led the authors to identify seven types of members.

TANNENBAUM, ARNOLD S. and KAHN, R. L. (1958). *Participation in Union Locals*. Evanston: Row, Peterson. An analysis of questionnaires completed by 761 members of 4 union locals in two American international trade unions.

TANNENBAUM, FRANK (1952). *A Philosophy of Labor*. New York: Knopf. (Republished 1964 as *The True Society: a Philosophy of Labour*. London: Cape.)

THOENES, PIET (1966). *The Elite in the Welfare State*. London: Faber and Faber. Part II is largely concerned with the role of politicians and administrators in the British system.

TRADES UNION CONGRESS (1970). *Report of 102nd Annual Trades Union Congress*. London: T.U.C.

TRADES UNION CONGRESS (1966). *Trade Unionism: The Evidence of the Trades Union Congress to the Royal Commission on Trade Unions and Employers' Associations*. London: T.U.C.

TRADES UNION CONGRESS (1955). *Women in the Trade Union Movement*. London: T.U.C. A historical account of women at work and as potential and active members of trade unions.

TURNER, HERBERT A., CLACK, G. and ROBERTS, G. (1967). *Labour Relations in the Motor Industry*. London: Allen and Unwin. A study of strikes and disputes in terms of technical change in the British motor car industry, 1948-1964.

ULMAN, L. (1961). 'Unionism and Collective Bargaining in the Modern Period' in SEYMOUR E. HARRIS, ed. *American Economic History*. New York: McGraw-Hill. Covers American trade unionism, etc. from 1933-1959.

VALL, VAN DE, MARK (1970). *Labor Organizations*. Cambridge University Press. A study, based on surveys in Dutch trade unions, labour party and co-operative movement.

WALTON, RICHARD E. and MCKERSIE, ROBERT E. (1965). *A Behavioural Theory of Labor Negotiations*. New York: McGraw-Hill. An analysis in terms of goals and tactics in the interaction between management and union representatives.

WARMINGTON, W. A. (1960). *A West African Trade Union*. London: Oxford University Press. A study of organization of and disputes between the Workers' Union of the Camaroons Development Corporation and the management of the Corporation.

WEBB, SIDNEY and BEATRICE (1894). *The History of Trade Unionism*. London: Longmans.

WEBB, SIDNEY and BEATRICE (1898). *Industrial Democracy*. London: Longmans. An analysis of the structure and functioning of British trade unions in a historical framework, a supplement to their *History*.

WEBB, SIDNEY and BEATRICE (1935). *Soviet Communism: a New Civilization?* London: S. and B. Webb. Chapter 3 deals with trade unionism and collective bargaining.

WEBER, MAX (1958). *The City*. New York: Free Press. Chapter 4 deals with the Italian guild controlled cities.

WEDDERBURN, KENNETH W. (1965). *The Worker and the Law*. Harmondsworth: Penguin Books. Chapters 7-10 deal with industrial conflict, strikes, trade unions and members' rights.

WIGHAM, ERIC (1961). *What's Wrong with the Unions?* Harmondsworth: Penguin Books. A journalist's criticism of British trade unionism.

WILENSKY, HAROLD L. (1956). *Intellectuals in Labor Unions.* Glencoe, Illinois: The Free Press. A study of professional employers in 28 American union headquarters.

WILENSKY, HAROLD L. (1965). 'The Problems and Prospects of the Welfare State' in WILENSKY and LEBAUX, CHARLES N. *Industrial Society and Social Welfare.* New York: Free Press, Paperback Education. The introduction to the paperback edition of this book discusses American welfare in the control of the welfare states.

WOOTTON, BARBARA (1955). *The Social Foundations of Wage Policy.* London: Allen and Unwin. Chapter 5 contains an analysis of cases submitted to the National Arbitration Tribunal and the Industrial Court, 1940-1949.

Index

135